Teaching Traveller Children
maximising learning outcomes

Teaching Traveller Children
maximising learning outcomes

Patrick Alan Danaher, Phyllida Coombes
and Cathy Kiddle

Trentham Books
Stoke on Trent, UK and Sterling, USA

Trentham Books Limited

Westview House	22883 Quicksilver Drive
734 London Road	Sterling
Oakhill	VA 20166-2012
Stoke on Trent	USA
Staffordshire	
England ST4 5NP	

First published 2007

British Library Cataloguing-in-Publication Data
A catalogue record for this book is available from the British Library

Cover photographs by Cathy Kiddle

ISBN: 978 1 85856 377 0

Designed and typeset by Trentham Print Design Ltd, Chester and printed in Great Britain by Hobbs the Printers Ltd, Hampshire.

Contents

Glossary of Acronyms

ACERT Advisory Council for the Education of Romanies and other Travellers

DES Department of Education and Science

DfE Department for Education

DfEE Department for Education and Employment

DfES Department for Education and Skills

EAL English as an Additional Language

EFECOT European Federation for the Education of the Children of Occupational Travellers

E-LAMP E-Learning and Mobility Project

HMI Her Majesty's Inspectorate/Inspector

HMSO Her Majesty's Stationery Office

ICT Information and Communications Technology

LEA Local Education Authority

LGR Local Government Reorganisation

NATT National Association of Teachers of Travellers

NGEC National Gypsy Education Council

Ofsted Office for Standards in Education

SATs Standard Assessment Tasks

TES Traveller Education Service

TESS Traveller Education Support Service

Acknowledgments

For all teachers

Learning is our core purpose and that is what makes us human – the promise of education must include every learner and every educator, and we must continue to find ways to position them at the centre of the learning agenda, the curriculum, the life and soul of our school[s], colleges and universities (Currie, 2006, p837)

Education needs to learn to value its human face over its organisational one, and teachers need to be at the vanguard. (Leaton Gray, 2006, p170)

The research for this book is based on interviews with heads of service and teachers from various English Traveller Education Support Services. They gave unstintingly of their time and interest and shared significant aspects of their identities and strategies, in many cases to someone they had not met before. Without them this book would not have been possible. Our thanks to

Lucy Beckett	Helen Blow	John Burkinshaw
Lesley Clay	Jean Compton	Linda Corfield
Kathleen Cresswell	Helen Currie	Richard Foster
Nigel Groom	Pat Holmes	Margaret Holt
Jeanne Kenyon	Cathy Kiddle	Janet Mascarenhas
Vicki Redford	John Ryan	Jennifer Sanderson
Peter Saunders	Margaret Small	Margaret Telfer
Chris Tyler	Linda Walker	Dawn Warr
David Williams	Malcolm Wilson	

Phyllida Coombes and Geoff Danaher transcribed the interview tapes professionally and uncomplainingly, even when espresso machines in the background made the process difficult.

The authors have benefited enormously from reading the publications about Traveller education, many of them published by Trentham Books and written by some of the educators named above. Other teachers involved in Traveller education, particularly

Anne Walker, Ginny Harrison-White and Marion Rowlands, have helped ensure that the text is up to date and accurate.

At Trentham Books, Gillian Klein has been encouraging and supportive and has shown faith in the project from the outset, while insisting appropriately that the book should be of practical use to educators as well as being underpinned by theoretically in-formed research; her editorial expertise has enhanced the text's clarity and readability. Her colleagues have likewise been approachable and helpful.

Arthur Ivatts' pioneering work as inspector, adviser and supportive colleague over many years has been a significant inspiration for many Travellers and educators alike; the authors are grateful to him for writing the Foreword to the book.

Funding to conduct the research reported in the book was provided by the then Faculty of Education and Creative Arts at Central Queensland University in Australia, as part of Patrick Danaher's sabbatical leave. Patrick has been sustained by his doc-toral supervisors, Leo Bartlett and Leonie Rowan; by Geoff Danaher, Peter Hallinan, Ian Kindt, Beverley Moriarty, Colin Rose, Rob Thompson and Doug Wyer, the current and former members of the Traveller education research team; and by interested col-leagues and kindred spirits there and in the Faculty of Education and the Centre for Research in Transformative Pedagogies at the University of Southern Queensland. We are also grateful to the Travellers, educators and researchers in Australia, Ireland, Italy, the Netherlands, Nigeria, the UK and Venezuela who broadened the understandings in this book.

As always, it is the family and personal relationships that have provided greatest motivation at times of stress and trial: we thank you all unreservedly for your support.

Foreword

Arthur Ivatts, OBE

In the early 1970s I was a postgraduate research student at Hull University. My thesis focused on the ethnography of the Gypsies of East Yorkshire and included a study of their response to social and educational provision. At that time 40 per cent of the nomadic families in the Hull and East Yorkshire area were in horse-drawn wagons. The action research started with the establishment of a voluntary school with 60 students of all ages. It was not long before the organisers wisely asked the local education authority (LEA) to visit the school. Following some initial hesitations, the East Riding Education Authority accepted full responsibility for the provision. In hindsight, of course, it was segregated and discriminatory provision which thankfully would be totally unacceptable today.

This early personal experience of work in Traveller education, with its close association with the establishment of one of the earliest Traveller Education Support Services (TESS), provides me with perhaps a unique advantage in writing the foreword to this immensely interesting book on the work of TESSs, their personnel and their contextual interface and encounters with other key players in education.

The work of TESSs has frequently been commended, and particularly so by Her Majesty's Inspectors of Schools, for the quality and sustainability of the professional activities in relation to the support for Gypsy, Roma and Traveller students and their schools, and the development of trusting relationships with the families. These positive assessments have been well-founded on the evidence. This book adds much to our understanding of the professional people involved, their backgrounds and their personal motivations. The story told here about the professionalism of a small group of dedicated and tenacious people is one that must be told because it not only provides a description of a unique educational development but also goes some way in providing future Gypsy, Roma and Traveller scholars with the evidence that the historic racist abuse towards their communities was mitigated by some bright lights of hope and justice.

The story thus told illustrates graphically the reality that TESS coordinators and their close team colleagues have worked tirelessly over the last 30 years in virtually uncharted professional waters, and – to extend the metaphor – that they have constantly had to battle against the waves of limited and threatened resources, ignorance, discrimination and blatant race hatred. These efforts have not been without their tensions but, even in the context of competition for scarce resources, cooperation and solidarity have been the dominant professional ingredients that have ensured the continuing will to secure justice and respect for the Traveller children and their families.

The relationships between the TESSs and Traveller children and their families are well described in this book. They reveal an abundance of the skills demanded to establish trusting and respectful relationships with communities which have learnt to survive prejudice and discrimination over centuries. The relationships with schools and teachers provide a telling picture of the multiplicity of survival skills required of the TESS personnel in terms of keeping an eye on the goal of raising the achievement of Traveller children through an impressive adaptability to any situation.

The professional work of TESS within the political and administrative contexts of central and local government policies towards Gypsy and Traveller communities is carefully crafted, with balance and wise judgment, but there are nonetheless sections that should make for uncomfortable reading for anyone with an uneasy conscience about injustice, racism and discrimination.

Teaching Traveller Children: maximising learning outcomes should serve as a work of practical reference for policy-makers as well as the academic specialist in education, who would be well advised to note the evidence that quite special professional people are needed in situations which place unique demands on professional skills, and especially so in a context where the client groups have a very low public esteem. All readers irrespective of motivation will benefit from its objectivity, balance and accuracy. This is a book based on the welcome transformative research approach and it is relevant and up to date. The sections at the end of each chapter devoted to implications for practice will make a valuable contribution to the knowledge base of policy, provision and practice related to the education of Traveller communities.

Introduction

This introduction sets out the context in which TESS teachers are working. It gives a brief history of the development of the Services and the current working situation. Locating the book in the Traveller education literature, it outlines the research project and the book's organisation.

eaching Traveller Children is concerned with the work of the heads of service and teachers who staff the English Traveller Education Support Services (TESSs). The TESSs function to facilitate the educational success of learners who for reasons of ethnicity and/or mobility call themselves or are called 'Travellers'. These groups include:

- Gypsy Travellers (on authorised or unauthorised sites, or recently in housing)
- Irish and Scottish Travellers
- Fairground Travellers
- Circus Travellers
- New Travellers
- Roma (Gypsy Travellers from Eastern Europe)
  (see also Currie and Danaher, 2001, p34; O'Hanlon and Holmes, 2004, pp3-14).

The responsibilities of the educators in TESSs are complex and diverse, combining the specialised roles of Traveller education with the increasingly demanding and politicised duties of mainstream teachers. This is evident in the groups and institutions with which the TESSs have sustained contact:

- Traveller children
- Traveller families
- other members of TESSs

- ▪ local schools, including headteachers, administrators, classroom and support teachers and students
- ▪ the Department for Education and Skills
- ▪ the LEAs
- ▪ other departments and agencies within local authorities
- ▪ other government and non-government welfare agencies
- ▪ members of the general public (see also Danaher *et al*, 2002, pp20-21)

The book is focused on two key elements of these educators' work: their professional and personal identities. It examines the strategies that they deploy to maximise the learning outcomes of Traveller children. We found a direct and iterative relationship between these elements: the educators' insights into the character of Traveller education and their understandings of their own capabilities and limitations as educators help to facilitate the effectiveness of the strategies that they use, and that effectiveness in turn refines and reinforces their self-perceptions and identities.

The English Traveller Education Support Services

The TESSs in England have evolved in piecemeal fashion over the past three decades (Binns, 1990), although there were earlier efforts at legislation such as between 1900 and 1940 relating to children living on canal boats (Bowen, 2001). It became evident to government, particularly through a Schools Council research study (Reiss, 1975), that it was insufficient for LEAs simply to operate open door policies in respect of Traveller children. One case, which caught national attention, demonstrated that not every LEA was opening the door. In 1977 a young Traveller, Mary Delaney, was refused admission to a school in Croydon by the local authority because she came from an unauthorised site; that is, her family had no legal place to live and were camping on the side of the road. Two Gypsy support organisations, the Advisory Council for the Education of Romany and Other Travellers (ACERT) and the National Gypsy Education Council (NGEC) mounted strong protests at this denial of a basic right and threatened to take action in the European Court. The pressure met with success in that the 1980 Education Act and the Department of Education and Science Circular 1/81 made it quite clear that an Authority's duties to make school places available extended to every child: 'The reference to children 'in the area' of the Authority means that each Authority's duty extends to all children residing in their area, whether permanently or temporarily. The duty thus embraces in particular travelling children, including Gypsies' (DES, 1981, clause 5).

Even when the door was open, however, more proactive policies were needed to encourage Traveller families to enter the formal education system. The government put in place a series of funding mechanisms to enable LEAs to provide extra support for Traveller children where this was necessary for them to achieve equal opportunities. The result was that from the early 1980s LEAs individually began to establish TESSs.

There were, however, no specific guidelines or minimum performance standards for the operation of Traveller education projects. Travellers are a highly sensitive political issue and, as with the accommodation issue – the provision of enough sites – successive governments have failed to grasp the nettle. They did not clarify the particular role that TESSs should play within any kind of national strategy. The result was that LEAs developed their various projects separately, with different levels of provision at different times and at different speeds. They responded to local circumstances, locally based Traveller groups and travelling patterns, within the financial constraints imposed by their individual budgets. A few LEAs cooperated to provide consortium services, but there was and is no national consistency.

The TESSs established earliest tended to work initially only with Gypsy Traveller and Irish Traveller groups, who had the greatest perceived needs in terms of access to education. Provision became more varied and sophisticated as the needs of fairground and circus families were later identified, then those of New Travellers. Recently Roma families from Eastern Europe were added to the client groups.

TESSs have moved through various stages of development, from teaching Traveller children at the roadside, to operating mobile schools as bridging arrangements to ease access into schools, and subsequently to working much more as support agencies with families and schools, emphasising that the main responsibility for the children's education lies with the schools exactly as for all other children. The trend for Traveller Education Services (TESs) to rename themselves as Traveller Education Support Services (TESSs) marked this philosophical change.

At the time of the interviews on which this book is based (1999), TESSs were funded by three-year project grants, awarded through a competitive bidding system. After 2002 the Traveller specific grants were subsumed into a larger grant for services to 'vulnerable children'. No longer was Traveller education funding ring-fenced, but local authorities were expected to consider their needs alongside others deemed vulnerable.

LEAs themselves changed, as the Children Act 2004 (HMSO, 2004) demanded that local authorities merge aspects of education and social services to create multidisciplinary children's services and produce a children and young people's plan. This trend to a more horizontal means of provision has moved Traveller education towards the mainstream, yet has created an environment in which their particular needs may be lost.

TESS staff have had to change their roles and realign their services as the educational terrain has changed. Services are still expected to give support to families and children in school, but also they are expected to offer more and more training – for teachers in schools, for colleagues in other agencies and to the emerging Children's Services Teams. All this with no budget increase.

More broadly, during the 30 years of Traveller education covered in this book, the government department responsible for education has changed its name from the Department for Education and Science (DES) to the Department for Education (DfE) to the Department for Education and Employment (DfEE) to the current Department for Education and Skills (DfES). We use the acronym of the time we are discussing.

An acknowledgment of the challenges currently presented to TESSs came in a conference called by the Department for Education and Skills in March 2006, 'Let's Discuss the Best Way Forward'. The conference was intended to celebrate the work of TESSs and to think ahead, and generated a Department for Education and Skills (2006) guidance paper entitled *Positive Pathways for the Future of Provision for Gypsy, Roma and Traveller Children*.

Consideration of the professional and personal challenges to TESS staff, past and future, is at the heart of this book. We hope it will make a contribution to the debate and add our voices to the celebration of their achievements.

The literature on Traveller Education
This section reviews the field of literature to which the book aspires to contribute – Traveller education – but is by no means exhaustive. Significant themes are identified in the literature that resonate with and help to frame our own arguments.

The Traveller education literature is currently undergoing a flowering, after decades in which Travellers were either absent from educational research or portrayed as unfortunate victims of an unnatural lifestyle if they were included in such research (Danaher, 2001a, chapter two). This welcome shift can be summarised as the literature's representations of Travellers moving from *deficit* and *disadvantage* to *difference* to *diversity*.

We welcome this shift and are influenced by contemporary theorising of mobility. Noting 'the inclination to view itinerant groups predominantly as down and out riff-raff' (p2), Lucassen, Willems and Cottar (1998) asserted:

> Our knowledge has been severely restricted not only because of historical negligence, but also because of two closely connected paradigms, one which views Gypsies and other itinerant groups as criminal, marginal and poor, and another which focuses almost exclusively on their alleged common ethnic identity and origin. (p2)

McVeigh (1997) persuasively defined sedentarism 'as that system of ideas and practices which serves to normalise and reproduce sedentary modes of existence and pathologise and repress nomadic modes of existence' (p9). Drawing on historical analysis of the lengthy provenance of commonly expressed assumptions and stereotypes about Travellers, for example in the transition to agriculture, the fall of the Roman Empire and the move to industrialisation, McVeigh argued that the 'romanticised' and 'pathologised' constructions of Travellers are equally destructive:

> It is wrong to use notions which reproduce the dichotomy between 'good' Travellers (ethnic, exotic, romantic, free) and bad travellers (non-ethnic, dispossessed and debased sedentaries, subcultures of poverty). In fact, the suggested dichotomy between the construction of the romanticised 'Raggle Taggle Gypsy' and the pathologised 'itinerant' is a false one. Both simultaneously inform contemporary ideas about, and the treatment of, *all* nomadic peoples. (p15; emphasis in original)

Thus most previous and some current depictions of Travellers derived from this fundamental ambivalence about their mobility. Whether that mobility is celebrated because of its exoticism or feared because it detaches itinerant people from the privileges and responsibilities of living in permanently settled communities, the result is the same: mobility deviates from the norm of fixed residence, and that deviation causes educational problems that systems have to redress. We argue that diversity holds the key to moving beyond this limited and limiting understanding of Travellers: highlighting the diversity across and within Traveller communities draws attention to the multiple dimensions of their subjectivities and of the lived experiences that make them human. This approach is both anti-sedentarist (Danaher *et al*, 2004), because it seeks to disrupt the pathologising of nomadic modes of existence (McVeigh, 1997), and anti-essentialist (Danaher, 2001b), because it declines to essentialise mobile communities by defining them purely or even primarily in terms of their mobility.

We have used this approach to reconceptualising mobility as a lens for viewing the Traveller education literature as it relates to England. In that context, the Plowden Report, *Children and Their Primary Schools* (DES, 1967), was one of the earliest British government references to Gypsy Travellers, whom it designated 'Britain's most educationally deprived group', estimating that fewer than 10 per cent of eligible children attended school. Evoking the dominant discourse of deficit and disadvantage about Travellers at the time, Adams and Smith (1967), whose synthesis of educational research was included in the Plowden Report, noted:

> ... although the group of [Gypsy Traveller] children involved is too small to justify a discussion of this length in the body of our Report, the children's educational needs are nevertheless extreme and largely unmet. Moreover the economic and social handicaps of the group from which they come arise to a large extent from the fact that successive generations of gipsy [sic] children are deprived of the education that would enable them to compete on equal terms with the rest of the community. Extreme as they are, the needs of gipsy children cannot be effectively met by measures of the kind we recommend for the more general problems of urban deprivation. (p595)

Despite the references to 'extreme', 'handicaps' and 'deprived', this statement contained a recognition of the Travellers' specialised educational needs arising from their ethnicity and/or mobility and constituted the seeds of appropriately specialised support that came to fruition with the establishment of the TESSs. More extensive coverage of Travellers was given at the time in Reiss's (1975) report of the Schools Council Project on the Education of Travelling Children that he had directed (Derrington and Kendall, 2004, p3; Kiddle, 1999, p26). Reiss cautioned against the automatic ascription of the label 'disadvantaged' to Travellers: 'Though Travellers often reveal classic symptoms of severe social and cultural deprivation, they cannot easily be placed within the general spectrum of the disadvantaged. Their unique and fascinating case presents a very real challenge to teachers and administrators' (p8).

A 1983 discussion paper on Traveller education from the Department of Education and Science was followed two years later by the Swann Report, *Education for All* (DES, 1985), which focused on the education of ethnic minority learners. The recognition of Travellers' specialised educational needs was evident, for reasons of both ethnicity and mobility, but it was also clear that ten years on from Reiss's (1975) report little had changed in terms of the access and achievement of Traveller children.

The shift from deficit and difference to diversity is seen clearly in the published work of the third author of this book. Cathy Kiddle (1981) used her account of living in a caravan to work for a touring theatre company to emphasise the fundamental link between mobility and the lack of educational provision. In *Traveller Children: A Voice for Themselves* (Kiddle, 1999), she drew on her extensive experience as Coordinator of the Devon Consortium TES to highlight and promote the diversity and heterogeneity within Traveller communities. In particular, she traced negative educational experiences to the prevailing discriminatory stereotypes ascribed to Travellers, yet she also demonstrated the mutual benefits accruing from positive educational experiences based on reciprocal trust and understanding between Travellers and teachers (see also Kiddle, 2000).

Similarly, Chris Derrington and Sally Kendall's (2004) book *Gypsy Traveller Students in Secondary Schools: Culture, Identity and Achievement* presented the findings of the first British national longitudinal study of Gypsy Travellers in secondary schools. It used a phenomenological research design to articulate the complex and multiple connections among the students' cultural backgrounds, their identities and their educational achievement. Although Derrington and Kendall succeeded in emphasising the heterogeneity of Traveller culture, their concluding note was pessimistic: '... evidence from this study has shown that Traveller students are still under-achieving, are still more likely to be excluded and are still liable to encounter racism within the school context' (p183). This suggests that sedentarism, like most if not all forms of othering and forces of marginalisation, is both intricately associated with formal education and highly resistant to transformative alternatives.

Other research confirms the intensity of prejudice experienced by Traveller children, the complexity of interconnecting factors which affect their educational achievement and the difficult task facing TESS staff. O'Hanlon and Holmes (2004) presented an overview of Traveller groups, current educational practice and legislation arising from a staff development course, demonstrating the need for continual professional development for teachers who are themselves often working in isolated and marginalised circumstances.

The emphasis of *Traveller Education: Accounts of Good Practice* (Tyler, 2005) was likewise on articulating those actions that helped to make a difference in Travellers' academic attainment. These ranged from supporting early years education and boosting formal literacy and numeracy skills to easing the transition from primary to secondary schooling and facilitating distance learning. We return to these publications and also to *Traveller Children: A Voice for Themselves* (Kiddle, 1999) where relevant.

This is a brief review of the literature about Traveller education in England. The significant work in Scotland (eg Jordan, 2000) and Ireland (eg Kenny, 1997; Sullivan, 2006) is noted but is outside the brief of this project, as is equivalent work with the children of seasonal workers in Mexico and the southern United States (eg Gouwens, 2001; LeBlanc Flores, 1996) and with nomadic pastoralists in Africa, Asia and Australia (eg Dyer, 2006). We have identified a general shift in conceptualising Travellers from deficit and disadvantage to difference to diversity, while acknowledging the resilience of sedentarist attitudes in some quarters in relation to Traveller education. This book looks for evidence of both that shift and that resilience in the recorded words and stated actions of the heads of service and teachers from several TESSs who participated in the study. It uses the connections between those educators' identities and strategies and the maximisation of Travellers' learning outcomes to make some broader points about contemporary educational practice.

The research project

The research reported in the book consisted of 22 semi-structured interviews conducted by Patrick with 26 (eighteen female and eight male) heads of service and teachers in nineteen TESSs between early March and early July 1999. These interviews resulted in over 200,000 words of transcripts, mostly transcribed by Phyllida, and were part of a broader project that yielded more than 500,000 words of transcripts and that included interviews with Travellers – barge, circus and fairground people – educators, policy-makers and community members in Belgium, the Netherlands, the UK and Venezuela. The Services ranged from metropolitan London and the rural southwest to the industrial midlands and the regional northwest, and the participants included people who had worked in Traveller education for decades as well as those who were new to it.

The currency of the attitudes and perceptions conveyed in the research has been updated and enhanced in two ways. Firstly, Patrick has maintained close contact since the interviews with several of the participants. Secondly, Cathy, who also participated in the research and who for over twenty years was in charge of a large TESS covering three LEAs, engaged in extensive discussions in 2005 and 2006 with former colleagues about changes to Traveller education since the interviews were conducted. She has also been responsible for highlighting at the end of each chapter the links between the interview data and current practice. And her Masters degree research (Kiddle, 2004) into the leadership and management of TESSs contributes to the book's conceptual framework.

The original goal had been to conduct interviews with as many different groups of Travellers as possible, mainly in the UK but also in Continental Europe. However, it became clear from the early interactions with Betty Jordan, then Director of the Scottish Traveller Education Project at the University of Edinburgh, and with Cathy, then Coordinator of the Devon Consortium TES, that it was both unrealistic and unfair to ask these and other intermediaries to set up interviews between Travellers with whom they had built up rapport and trust over many years and an Australian researcher who was unknown to those Travellers. So even though several interviews were conducted with the aforementioned barge, circus and fairground people, the focus of the research was enlarged to include the work and identities of educators who work with Travellers.

The selection of these educators as potential participants in the research was contingent and situated rather than strategic or systematic. Patrick began by organising interviews with educators with whom he had had contact, but they suggested colleagues who might be interested, and the research expanded. Interviews were mostly conducted once only with one head of service or teacher each time, although Cathy was interviewed twice and a few participants were interviewed in pairs. The length of interviews varied widely, according to the participants' availability. Most took place in the respective TESS and a few in more social settings.

This phase of the project aimed first to understand the participants' constructions of their working lives – the aspirations, constraints, possibilities, experiences and outcomes that animated and motivated their approach to what they generally accepted were complex and demanding roles. The second aim was to elicit the kinds of educational strategies they deployed and the perceived effectiveness of those strategies in making a difference in the lives of their Traveller students.

The questions posed during the interviews developed over time, with a rather generalised set of questions at the outset giving way to an accumulated enquiry that drew on reflections on participants' input in previous interviews. One example was the perceived significance and influence of the 1994 Criminal Justice and Public Order Act; another was the problems and possibilities presented by the recently implemented literacy hour.

The research design underpinning the collection and analysis of the data was qualitative, interpretivist, phenomenological and poststructuralist (Somekh and Lewin, 2005). That is, we were interested in understanding the participants' words as reflections of their constructions of and engagements with the lived experiences of being heads of service and teachers in particular English TESSs, while recognising that those constructions and engagements were influenced by broader manifestations of sociocultural, economic and political forces. The focus was on narrative constructions and highlighting participant and researcher reflexivity.

The interpretation of the participants' words drew on textual and thematic analysis in order to conduct a form of ongoing dialogue between their and the authors' voices, with Cathy in the dual role of participant and author. Like Gale and Densmore (2003, p12) we highlighted the voices of research participants – that is, linking what they say with where and how they are positioned in relation to such broader issues as power structures. It accorded also with Rowan's (2001) elaboration of transformative textual analysis, whereby texts, including semi-structured interview transcripts, are subjected to such questions as who and what are included and excluded, what is represented as natural and normal and who and what are valued (p47). In other words, meaning is in a continuing process of reconstruction and renegotiation, for example through dialogue between interviewee and interviewer and among the authors of this book.

Finally and perhaps most importantly, we have attended to the ethical and political dimensions of conducting and publishing the research. Quoted opinions and statements have not been ascribed to individual participants and TESSs and we have tried to be as respectful as possible to the participants while reserving the right to present our interpretation of their words and stated actions. This is not simply to carry out customary practice in qualitative research; it is to recognise that Traveller educators, like Traveller communities, are at once marginalised and politicised. These twin dimensions of the work of Traveller educators are manifested in a wide range of issues, from bidding for funding and the allocation of resources to naming and recognition by LEAs.

These ethical and political dimensions of the research have prompted our aspiration that the book will display at least some of the features of Anyanwu's (1998) definition of transformative research:

> Transformative research is a systematic enquiry into the real conditions which create oppression or hinder self-determination. It produces reflective knowledge which helps people to identify their situation and in doing so, to change such [a] situation for the better. In this regard, transformative research plays the important role of supporting the reflective process that promotes positive change. (p45)

We hoped to do this in two ways. First, by communicating to a wider audience, particularly of other educators, the educational strategies the heads of service and teachers of the TESSs have developed and deployed for teaching Traveller children during years, sometimes decades, of experience. Second, by linking the effectiveness or otherwise of those strategies to broader issues of the situated and politicised character of contemporary educational practice, thereby helping to open that practice to critique and to hold it to account.

The book

The book is divided into five parts, each with two chapters and each elaborating a different location in the Traveller educator's world. Part 1 focuses on the educators themselves, analysing their constructions of themselves and one another as constituting a specialised field of teachers' work. In Part 2, we turn to Traveller sites, highlighting the participants' perceptions of their relations with Traveller children and their parents and families. Part 3 deals with government and LEAs, specifically the participants' experiences of policies from these two arenas of policy-making. Part 4 concentrates on the participants' relations with the headteachers and teachers of the primary and secondary schools concerned. Finally, Part 5 considers Traveller education as sites of innovative curriculum practice, and we chose teaching literacy and the use of educational technologies as two pedagogical elements where Traveller educators are particularly adept and skilled. The conclusion to the book synthesises the main themes canvassed in the text and returns to reconsider the issues identified in this introduction from the perspective of the intervening analysis.

Each chapter begins by locating the participants' words in the broader context of a key element of teachers' work and identities. The centrepiece of the chapters is an analysis of their attitudes and stated actions in relation to the issue for examination, with an appropriate spread of interviews across the ten chapters and the interviews identified by the order in which they were conducted. Each chapter concludes by identifying the implications of these attitudes and actions for teachers' practice and professional development. Thus our focus is on the interplay between the educational strategies and the professional and personal identities of the heads of service and teachers, and how that interplay maximises Travellers' learning outcomes.

Part 1:
Traveller education heads of service and teachers

1
Constructions of selves

*What kind of person chooses to work in Traveller education and why
do so many of them stay for so long? Working with marginalised
groups can sometimes bring that marginalisation to the teachers
themselves. This chapter explores their qualities and motives, their
satisfactions and frustrations, and the importance of teamwork as a
survival strategy.*

Like the Traveller education literature, the scholarly field concerned with
teachers' work has undergone a considerable expansion in recent years.
We have taken from this extensive and rapidly growing field certain
themes that articulate with the purpose of this book and help to frame our
analysis of the participants' words.

In particular, we have been influenced by poststructuralist understandings of
identity and the self. These understandings are in keeping with the anti-
essentialist approach to conceptualising mobility noted in the introduction.
From this perspective, identity is perceived not as a fixed, unified pheno-
menon but rather as multiple and sometimes conflicting subjectivities that
are contingent and constructed and that are enacted and situated in specific
politicised contexts of place or space and time (Harreveld, 2002; McDougall,
2004). This focus is consistent with Weedon's (1987, p32; cited in McDougall,
2004, p95) definition of subjectivity as 'the conscious and unconscious
thoughts and emotions of the individual, her sense of herself and her ways of
understanding her relation to the world'. Thus teachers' subjectivities and
constructions of selves are a complex combination of elements – professional
and personal, public and private, formal and informal – all competing for

attention and affirmation in the daily lives and lived experiences of those educators.

This focus on teachers' subjectivities accords with Woods and Jeffrey's (2002) helpful synthesis of current ideas about teachers' identity work. They note that the unified notion of identity ascribed at the time of the Plowden Report (1967) has given way to a much more disaggregated, even fractured, set of subjectivities and an ongoing negotiation among competing discourses – or what Harreveld (2002) called 'discursive dissonance' (p105). This approach certainly accords with Hall's (2004) view that '... notions of change and struggle can usefully inform our understanding of the nature of teachers' work in the first decade of a new century'.

Furthermore, a recent theme issue of the journal *Teachers and Teacher Education* (Anteliz *et al*, 2006a) explored the impact on educators' identities of working with learners variously constructed as marginalised; see also the theme issue of *Teachers and Teaching: Theory and Practice* devoted to 'Teachers' Lives' (Loughran and Kelchtermans, 2006a). With particular relevance to this book, Gobbo (2006) used her article in that theme issue to interrogate the educational role played by parents of circus and fairground children in Italy, focusing on the links and dissonances between enculturation and schooling for these mobile families. Gobbo asserted that, while the parents often proved effective in their pedagogical role, their effectiveness was generally not recognised by either the schooling system or broader society, so that both the parents and their children generally remained marginalised within that society. Similarly, Currie (2006), another participant in this study, constructed her response to the theme issue in terms of the intersections among 'minorities', 'margins', 'misfits' and 'mainstreams' that educators working with variously marginalised groups of learners have to confront – both for the learners and for themselves.

Sullivan (2006) used her Doctor of Philosophy thesis at the University of Limerick to record the changes to her work practices as she responded to abstract notions of equality and social justice being juxtaposed with the lived realities of her role as a Resource Teacher for Traveller children in Ireland. For example:

> As a result of undertaking my research I changed my practice to one of acknowledging and accepting the legitimacy of the Traveller children's different vocabulary and manner of enunciating words, in contrast to my initial practice of trying to persuade them to adopt the nuances of Standard English ... (p275)

She insisted that her changed work practices were both informed by and contributed to theory:

> In terms of theory, I submit that I have demonstrated the need for a concept of inclusion that transcends assimilation, which can reflect a denial of difference, and integration, which often seeks to eliminate difference. Diverse viewpoints need to be accommodated, as the interests of justice cannot be served through imposing the wishes of the dominant majority on the oppressed minority. (p291)

In this case, this intersection between practice and theory was central to Sullivan's efforts to construct a sense of self that was professionally and personally meaningful and that also sought to support her students' learning.

This selective review has highlighted the contemporary literature's anti-essentialist emphasis on conceptualising teachers' work and their constructions of themselves in terms of multiple and competing subjectivities and discourses and the complex and often contradictory links between the micro world of the educational setting and the macro world of policy development. Consequently, in looking in this book at the words and stated actions of the heads of service and teachers, we are interested in both social structure and human agency (Giddens, 1984) as they are enacted and evidenced in the working lives of those heads of service and teachers. That is, we see the subjectivities of the participants in the research as a series of ongoing negotiations – between self and other, micro and macro, individual and institutional or systemic – in which meaning-making is temporary and tentative rather than permanent and assured.

Therefore one way in which the book is intended to contribute to the literature on teachers' work is to analyse why the participating heads of service and teachers conduct their working lives as they do and make links between their words and actions and those of other educators, in order to represent some of the topologies in the terrain of current educational practice. The other way is to use the analysis and links as the basis for identifying and evaluating practical strategies for discharging the responsibilities and enhancing the profiles of contemporary educators and for maximising their students' learning outcomes.

Given the diversity of the different groups of people collectively labelled 'Travellers' and the complexity of funding arrangements, legislation and relations with schools and other service providers, it was appropriate to ask how the TESS heads of service and teachers constructed their professional and personal selves. This broader inquiry divided logically into three questions:

- How and why did you move into Traveller education?
- Why do you remain in Traveller education?
- How do you see yourself as an educator?

What was striking about the participants was the wide spectrum of occupational itineraries that they had followed before they entered Traveller education. Some had worked in urban and others in rural schools; one person had been a teacher with a travelling circus; another had done voluntary work with young offenders in drama workshops; yet another had been working with emotionally and behaviourally disturbed children; and someone else had trained to teach children with hearing impairments. Quite a few participants had worked in one form or another of special needs education, although they varied considerably in whether they saw Traveller education fitting within this classification.

One participant noted that he was able to draw on his current position in Traveller education from the fact of 'having [had] experience with working with different ethnic groups who have very different needs, often language-based needs' (Interview A). Another participant explained that, having taught several year levels in a primary school for some years, 'the [local education] authority was being encouraged to set up a Traveller Education Service in some way, so they gave me a secondment'; 'The opportunity arose and I was ready to do it' (Interview H). From that secondment of two days a week and working with eleven schools attended by about 50 Traveller students, her work had expanded six years later to managing a Service and visiting nearly 400 Travellers in 55 to 70 schools each year.

Another participant had seized the day:

> I saw an advert. The local authority ... were advertising for a coordinator to run the service. I'd never been involved with Travellers at all before that although I'd worked with ethnic minorities, but it looked interesting so I applied. (Interview K)

And another:

> ... was teaching as a class teacher in a school where the Travellers attended before there was funding for a Traveller teacher ... I'd worked with Traveller children in the class for about seven years, and I was very interested in the culture, but I'd actually had my second child and didn't want full-time teaching, and this came up as a part-time post. So ... it also served a purpose that I could be part-time. (Interview T)

This situation echoed another's recollection:

> I'd been in primary and enjoyed that, and moved to middle school [and] enjoyed the work there. I'd got to know and was well settled in that school, progressed and got

> a few scale points for extra duties. But I thought I was ready to do something else, and this post came up and sounded really interesting. So I applied and I got the post working for – it wasn't really a service then, it was Travellers' education ... There had been a previous person in the post who had been in for about five years, and then she'd left to get the deputy headship, so no one had been doing the job for two terms when I started. So it was really in a way picking up from what ... had [been] done before me, but rebuilding those kind[s] of networks and contacts. (Interview U)

So some participants in the research went into Traveller education because they had a particular interest in Traveller culture or in issues of social justice, while others took advantage of opportunities as they presented themselves to enter a new arena of work. This demonstrates that some of the most effective and well-regarded Traveller educators came into the field through happenstance and were able to bring to it their respective combinations of character, experience and skills. Moreover, this occupational mobility and the motivations underpinning it resonate with both the working itineraries of Travellers and the increasingly fluid and flexible patterns in contemporary teachers' work. They also recall the ongoing interplay between the micro of an individual TESS head's or teacher's lifeworld and the macro of the complex web of networks and systems in which that head or teacher is employed.

Having entered Traveller education for various reasons and in widely varying circumstances, TESS heads of service and teachers offered an equivalent spectrum of reasons for remaining in their positions. For example, one participant stated that the interpersonal relationships with Travellers were sustaining even if challenging, while engaging with schools and coping with bureaucracy were difficult:

> In fact, the personal thing, the confrontations I really enjoy. I don't find that so stressful. It's actually the bureaucracy which is really trying. Because it's not just dealing with the Traveller community and all their immense number of problems, but dealing with teachers who are under stress, headteachers who are under stress. So you're sort of in the middle somewhere with this. (Interview R)

Another participant was sustained in Traveller education by its very complexity: 'I think it's the very diversity of our particular work, in Travellers' education certainly, that keeps you going, and it's something that you're discovering new things every day, new people ... It's the diversity and meeting very different people' (Interview A). Or as a different participant summarised the situation: 'That is the joy of the job as well, that you never know what's coming next week'. (Interview P)

There were pros and cons in working with a small team of colleagues. On the one hand: 'Because ... it is such a small team ... it has been plagued with difficulties on the teaching side. When it's such a small team and you're trying to share out responsibilities within the team anyway, it's frustrating when you can't' (Interview J). On the other hand:

> The commitment really comes over ... I can see the same commitment within that team for the Travellers and wanting to do the very best to provide the best service. Even since I've been here seeing the change in a relatively young staff and relatively new to the job. In one extreme wanting to be everything to all of them, and then seeing the best way to serve this population is in this way. 'Yes, I can do that and I can help them to do that themselves.' It's fascinating. So I hope I am staying. I'll let you know. (Interview J)

Another interviewee asserted her 'fundamental belief in the benefits of having [an] education' and that 'it is possible to make a difference' (Interview M). She was well aware that: 'Unfortunately in this job something horrendous will happen, people will say awful things and it won't work so well. But we keep doing it because you have to keep doing it' (Interview M). There were nonetheless plenty of examples of positive outcomes to sustain her colleagues and herself:

> I think every time one of the team comes back in, or phones me up sometimes at the end of the day, and says, 'It was great today. So and so did this, participated in this lesson, produced something, went on a school trip. And the parents were delighted. Mum thought it was great, and the teachers thought that they were lovely'. That happens, and what that means is that all of these ancient, almost innate prejudices are being broken down. They got broken down that day because Johnny went on the trip [and] had a wonderful time. The teacher thought he was fantastic ... They produced a lovely bit of work. They had the class photograph and it all went well. And nobody said, 'Oh, my God, that Traveller child! It was a disaster'. That day prejudices were addressed; that day it broke down. That's what it is, and it happens on a daily basis. (Interview M)

How teachers see themselves as educators goes to the heart of their effectiveness in helping their Traveller students to learn. So self-perceptions function as the point of intersection between educators' identities and their educational strategies; confidence or doubts in one area tend to spill over into the other.

As we expected, the participants saw themselves as educators in various ways (see also Danaher, 2005). N drew a sharp contrast between charity and social justice, saying that '... there is a perception of the support services that it's do-gooding ladies who are being kind to these poor things' and her own construction of her job '... as a way of ... generalising the issues that I've been interested in which were of access ...'.

R saw herself as working in areas of education most likely to promote innovation:

> I have never taught full-time in mainstream schooling ... What I do now is just about as close to mainstream schooling as I want to get ... I think it's something about being on the cutting edge for me, and I think that's why I've always done the type of teaching I have done. I like to be on that edge.

When asked what his TESS's 'philosophy of Traveller education' was S said:

> To me it's about giving [Travellers] choices. It's not about getting them to settle or giving them exams; it's giving them the choice whether they continue with what they want to do – [whether] they continue within their culture or in the fairground or whether they do something else. Giving them the opportunity to make that choice. If you haven't had education, then you don't have that choice.

Q asserted that: 'I like a challenge and I am a finisher, I see things through to the end. But I like variety, and there can't be any other job that offers the variety and the opportunity'. And she attributed equal commitment and enthusiasm to others working in Traveller education, despite the recurring pressures and stresses:

> This job – I get fed up with it, just like everybody else does ... [A] lot of it's crisis management, and you want to get on with other things, and you've got to balance the two. But I think that everybody that's in Traveller education will probably tell you the same thing. I bet you haven't spoken to one person who isn't enthusiastic about what they're doing.

Finally, several participants pondered the degree of convergence and divergence between their roles and those of social workers, while recognising that education welfare officers combined elements of both professions. B commented:

> Yes, it is difficult because it would be so easy to be drawn into the social work side of it. But you have to keep reminding yourself that you're there for the education. Yes, of course, you have to be aware that social workers that have issues will come in, but you've got to be very strict with yourself, otherwise you can just get drawn in. Because you care so much for the families and you get to know them so well, and they become personal friends, but you've got to keep that distance. We're there for the education of the children, and if we can call in other agencies and say, 'I think perhaps you're better placed to do this', then this is what we have to do. But there are very grey areas, aren't there?

This ongoing tension between education and social work reflected the location of Traveller education at the intersection of several different and sometimes competing, even conflicting, pressures and priorities for Travellers and educators alike. These pressures and priorities in turn influenced the multiple ways in which TESS heads of service and teachers constructed their professional and personal selves. Some insisted on clear demarcation to protect their responsibilities from unrealistic expectation and expansion while others were willing to tolerate a more flexible and intangible interpretation of their roles. Both approaches supported Traveller students' learning, even though they entailed different judgments about the most efficient and sustainable ways of bringing that support about.

Implications for practice

Many of the heads of service and teachers who were interviewed in 1999 had already been in post for several years. By 2007, two or three have retired or moved to other work, but most are still in post or working in a TESS in another part of the country. What keeps them there?

They have had little in the way of national policy guidelines and in many cases have themselves had to devise, write and see local policies through complex local authority committee structures. From the early 1980s on there have been several changes in government funding mechanisms for Traveller education. The only constant has been a continuing uncertainty over budgets, never guaranteed for more than a year ahead, making planning and development work difficult and frustrating. Local politicians will never put the education of Gypsies and Travellers as a high priority when preparing budgets for which they are accountable to their electorate. The teachers working with the group considered 'most at risk in the education system' (Ofsted, 1999, main findings) are likely to find themselves in services which are themselves marginalised and of low status. And still they stay.

TESS staff require immense emotional energy. As this book demonstrates, TESS heads and teachers need to build good relationships at every level if they are to survive and succeed in their work. They often find themselves acting as buffers between Traveller families and the education system, each with their own expectations and demands, and soaking up the anxieties and frustrations of others. Sometimes they are diplomats with highly developed negotiating skills, finding pathways to access education for the children around the barriers which stand in the way of equal opportunities. At other times they are advocates working with a double brief. On the one hand, they are passionate spokespersons for education, talking with parents for hours, making the case for the children to be given the chance to develop their academic potential and be able to make life choices. On the other hand, they will be advocates for Traveller families, challenging stereotyping and prejudice, as they seek a fair chance for the children.

As they move between these roles, members of TESS teams must tread carefully in the territory of professional and personal commitment. Back in 1996 a report (Ofsted, 1996) commented that TESS staff were remarkably committed to their work and they do show a strong sense of social justice. Many have come from mainstream teaching through various forms of special needs work into work with Travellers. Once they have experienced the depth of prejudice against Travelling people and have seen the barriers to educational access and achievement, it is hard to turn away. There is so clearly a job to be done. Yet it is a job of facilitation, of encouraging and enabling others to shoulder their own responsibilities, not of doing it for them. This line is often hard for teachers of Travellers to draw. They see the children not just in the classroom but also at home in the context of family and culture.

TESS heads and teachers need soft skills to fulfil their relationship and management roles. They also need the professional skills of teachers, trainers and advisers, able to move across the phases of education. Within a week they may be expected to work with and support mainstream teachers in an infant, junior or secondary classroom, deliver training to headteachers and school governors or student teachers on initial teacher training programs and give presentations to fellow professionals in other departments and agencies. They may have to teach strictly to the demands of the national curriculum or spend time in resource development to create materials appropriate to the needs and circumstances of the students. The larger TESSs are able to separate out these roles to some degree, but in smaller services, or those with a wide geographical spread, individuals may have to perform all these tasks.

It takes strong people to undertake this multiplicity of roles and tasks, people who can work on their own initiative and be prepared to take difficult professional decisions in what can often be isolated circumstances. Yet most TESSs operate as teams so staff must also be team players, helping to take the work of their service forward in a coherent way. It is difficult to make a set of strong individual personalities gel as a team, but it is one of the most important tasks of the head of service. Policies and structures have to be in place, so that team members understand their roles and responsibilities, yet flexibility must be inbuilt so that staff can respond and adapt to the daily changes in locations and circumstances of their client groups. Team meetings have social as well as professional functions. They provide the opportunity for mutual support and sharing experience, together with the chance to reinforce the common objectives of the work for teachers who may be working alone for much of the time. The team meetings must also allow time for problems and conflicts to arise and be resolved, lest they fester in isolation.

Looking from the outside, it seems that the teachers working in Traveller education teams are specialists who have developed a particular kind of expertise. In career terms many consider that working in Traveller education is a dead end, with no way back into the mainstream. Maybe they stay in their jobs because there is nowhere else to go. In a small world there are few chances for promotion within the TESSs. Headteachers of schools look for new staff with up to date classroom experience and often say that Traveller education teachers have been 'out of the classroom', not appreciating perhaps how many classrooms they have been in, how many teachers they have worked with and observed and how many different kinds of groups they have taught. Rather than specialists they could be seen as supreme generalists, with a wide range of skills and subject knowledge and experience of every phase of education. They are flexible and creative, finding innovative solutions to complex problems and able to relate to children, teachers and parents alike – assets to any post in education.

But, as the interview data show, many of the heads of TESSs say that they have had a developing career within the same job, as changes in national education priorities and policies have necessitated that their roles and functions have expanded and changed. Work in Traveller education has offered a breadth of educational experience that few other jobs could give, and few seek to change them. There is a high stress factor in keeping up to date with the demands of educational change and making connections between new policy initiatives and opportunities for Traveller children, but the day-to-day variety and constant challenge of the jobs are a stimulation for many. The needs of Traveller children are clear to see, but there are no easy or short-term solutions. Those who stay working with the same families and groups over a period of years have the long-term satisfaction of seeing real development happening, though always tinged with the frustrations caused by inadequate and uncertain funding. The widening of access and increase in attendance and achievement are sometimes noticeable only from one generation to the next, but they bear witness to the years of struggle and concern and sheer tenacity of the TESS heads and teachers.

2

Relations with other
Traveller educators

*Teachers of Travellers often work in isolation, without the backup of
close colleagues or a staffroom. So the development of personal support networks is important, as are professional development opportunities. The formation of NATT came from this background and
persists for these purposes. Sharing experience, developing practice
from needs assessed and discussed on the ground – innovative and
often pioneering work in difficult circumstances – this is the stuff of
Traveller education. Conversely there can be tensions when policy
and practice differ from one local authority to another and Traveller
families experience different provision or levels of support as they
move around the country.*

The literature on teachers' work acknowledges both the value and the
necessity of educators developing strong professional relationships
with their colleagues as one way of enhancing their constructions of
themselves and hence indirectly of supporting their students' learning. As
McDougall (2004) noted:

> Another key element of understanding how teachers adapt to change is the impact
> of the teacher's social world. Individuals have different perceptions of themselves in
> relation to the particular groups with whom they interact. These 'reference groups'
> are groups that the individual uses for monitoring personal goals and values (Nias,
> 1987, p8). Reference groups change over time as the individual changes and as
> his/her multiple subjectivities adapt to changing circumstances. (Nias, 1987, p103)

Unlike the archetypal charismatic teachers in screen culture skilfully analysed by Ellsmore (2005), who pointed out that 'the assumption in many charismatic teacher films is that the only figure in the school who understands what makes these students tick is the go-it-alone maverick', real life teachers tend more and more to rely on their colleagues for affirmation and confirmation that they are well-intentioned and effective practitioners in an increasingly complex and demanding profession. This is particularly the case when that affirmation and confirmation are withheld by students and their parents, their line managers and headteachers, and the developers of accountabilities and policies that often seem irrelevant at best and threatening and controlling at worst (Leaton Gray, 2006).

This dependence on peers for encouragement and support is even more important when the teachers work with students variously identified as marginalised (Anteliz *et al*, 2006a; Gale and Densmore, 2003). For example, Brunetti (2006) analysed survey questionnaires and interviews with a group of experienced teachers working at the pseudonymised inner city Presidio Higher School in California to explore the participants' enactment of 'resilience under fire' (p812), a significant component of which was the support they received in their work, including that of colleagues. One teacher in the study summed it up:

> I think at Presidio ... [collegiality is] particularly important. And one of the things I loved about Presidio when I first got here was just working with other teachers that were creative and interested in developing new things and thoughtful, and really also had great relationships with students and cared about them quite a bit. (p820)

We have seen that TESSs vary widely in terms of their longevity and size, so the capacities of heads of service and teachers to call on their colleagues in their own and other TESSs for support are also varied. Yet it is equally clear that the 'accounts of good practice' (Tyler, 2005) provided by experienced Traveller educators in aspects of provision ranging from early years and secondary education to literacy and distance learning depend for their success on the same principles that underpin those educators' ongoing professional learning: collaboration, cooperation, partnerships and teamwork, as did the catalogue of crucial educational support services that O'Hanlon and Holmes (2004, pp38-40) ascribed to TESSs.

This is true also of Derrington and Kendall's (2004) investigation of fourteen TESSs working in sixteen LEAs. What emerged was the potential – even the likelihood – of TESS staff members being positioned in negative and invidious ways in the complex web of relationships linking schools, Traveller students and their parents. One respondent encapsulated tellingly the frustration experienced when this occurred:

> It is a tightrope ... I think mum is right at times, I think the school is right at times and I think the school is very wrong at times and I think mum gets the wrong end of the stick at times and I am in the middle ... (p86)

Where, then, will Traveller educators receive professional support and development if not from their fellow TESS heads of service and teachers?

At the national level, the formation of the National Association of Teachers of Travellers (NATT) in 1980 provided a much-needed framework for organised support for its members, advocacy for Travellers and lobbying of decision-makers at national and local levels. For example, much discussion was devoted at NATT's one-day conferences to identifying the most effective ways of engaging with the instances of discrimination against Traveller students prompted by the publication of league tables of schools' performance indicators (Kiddle, 1999, p50). This was a striking instance of the need for Traveller educators to band together to combat a situation that was likely to contradict their continuing efforts to maximise their students' learning outcomes.

The analysis of data pertaining to Traveller educators' relations with other TESS heads of service and teachers clustered logically around three types and levels of relationships:

- colleagues in one's own TESS (local level)
- other TESSs (county and regional level)
- NATT (national level)

Lack of space precludes reference here to the international level, particularly to the former European Federation for the Education of the Children of Occupational Travellers (EFECOT). However, Chapter 10 looks at the role of EFECOT in facilitating innovative practice connected with the use of educational technologies. It shows how international collaborations provided opportunities for at least some TESS staff members to enlarge their networks and contribute to innovative projects that fuelled their sense of playing a role in important educational work, thereby enhancing their sense of self and strengthening their professional identities.

Almost all participants in the research explicitly or implicitly identified the relationships with their colleagues in their own TESS as a significant influence on their constructions of their professional and personal selves and their effectiveness in teaching their Traveller students. This was inevitable, given the small size of most TESSs and hence the interdependent character of the respondents' work. TESSs functioned as nurturing and supportive 'reference groups' (Nias, 1987; cited in McDougall, 2004, p103) when the working goals and patterns of individual Traveller educators were aligned harmoniously and in sync with those of their immediate peers – a case of integrated and co-operative communities (Johnson and Johnson, 1998) rather than loose and uncoordinated sets of lone rangers.

It was also inevitable that a mixed picture emerged about the operation of these reference groups. There were many examples of members of closely knit TESSs supporting one another and achieving far more than might reasonably be expected, given the wide range of responsibilities and the competing pressures on their time and energy. But there were sometimes internal tensions and conflicts that reflected conflicting interpretations of what should receive priority attention as well as the stress caused when strategies appeared not to succeed as well as had been hoped.

What also emerged from the interview data was the burden borne by TESS heads of service as they strove to meld together a cohesive and flexible team that was sufficiently dynamic and resilient to respond to competing and constantly changing external and internal expectations. Though often achieved, this was sometimes at significant personal cost.

Several participants spoke explicitly about the necessity and value of effective teamwork within TESSs. According to R: 'We are at our most successful when we work together as a team, when the families know all of us, know what our roles are and where we fit in'. He added: 'I think we're extremely well-organised and, mainly because we're a relatively small team, although it is going to expand, we can work ... very closely. I think it's much more difficult with a widespread team'. Furthermore, when the elements of a successful team were clearly aligned, the outcome was the capacity to make localised, responsive decisions that had a considerable impact on students' learning:

> It's that kind of flexibility. We make choices. For example we've been working a little bit in preschool, and [a team member has] been involved in a Percentage for Arts project with some young people [about] photography. We got some funding from somewhere else to do that. Because we make our own choices, we look at where we feel the work would be most beneficial which isn't [sitting] in the classroom a lot of the time with the child. You need that, but you need a lot of other things to make that happen, to make that successful. (Interview K)

At the same time, there was a recognition that Traveller educators are not all equally well-suited to this kind of teamwork and that such work required particular attributes that were highly valued:

> And in a team like ours everything is shared ... Everything is shared, everything is open and we work very cooperatively together. Some people do that better than others, but again you need to be that kind of person who works with other people well. And not everybody does ... That's really difficult in this kind of team, where so much of the information needs to be shared. So much of what people are doing in terms of work can be shared. (Interview F)

Teamwork, then, is both crucial to success and difficult to achieve. It is crucial because resources, particularly human resources, are scarce and demands are considerable and competing – effective teamwork is the only possible strategy for negotiating that ongoing contradiction. It is difficult because human interaction is complex and uncertain and perhaps even more so in fields that throw into sharp relief questions of power, equity and social justice. So TESSs were certainly not invariably harmonious or necessarily models of functional teams. But those that were – and many were – also demonstrated successful learning outcomes for Traveller students.

Traveller educators displayed close and enduring relationships with heads of service and teachers in other TESSs. As with the situation within their own TESSs, this was largely a strategic response to necessity: TESSs were generally small and lacked the economies of scale and degrees of influence enjoyed by larger organisations. We found that this necessity was transformed into effective partnerships and successful educational practices on a surprisingly broad scale, particularly considering that teaching is generally regarded as an individual and sometimes lonely profession. The skills of teamwork devised within single TESSs were thereby generalised to the county or regional level.

Despite this positive outcome, a certain ambivalence was evident in some discussions about fellow TESSs. This ambivalence derived partly from the perception that services were competing with one another for scarce government funding and partly from an understandable diversity of views about the most effective ways of making a difference to Traveller students' learning outcomes. This divergence of thinking, sometimes evident within individual TESSs, was thus generalised to a broader level in a similar way to the teamwork skills identified above. It led to healthy and much-needed debate about a field that sometimes seemed to have more questions than answers. This was also evident at the national level, particularly in the operations of NATT.

There was certainly strong evidence that TESS heads of service used their knowledge of other TESSs as informal benchmarks against which to monitor and measure their own performance and effectiveness. This kind of un-official, even unconscious, comparison is a potentially useful feature of educational practice, particularly when learners are considered marginalised. We noted that when Traveller educators spoke about other TESSs they generally reflected on the reasons for the differences among TESSs. For example: 'That makes us different from other Traveller services because of the logistics. So we don't do the same kind of individual work with children that other services do, because logistically it's just not possible' (Interview F).

There was a high level of cooperation and sharing, and sometimes collabora-tion, among TESSs that was particularly helpful to new heads of service and heads of new TESSs. As H noted: 'Then I also visited other ... established Traveller services across the country to look at good practice'. This respondent was enthusiastic about the preparedness of TESS staff to share ideas and in-formation and the benefits of doing so:

> We run conferences, training days and so on, and I think we learn a lot from each other. Perhaps we're much more open with each other and share more than schools do ... We'd rather share our concerns and also the good things that we've learnt. (Interview H)

However, we found some tension and ambivalence in Traveller educators' relations with other TESSs. Despite the cooperation and collaboration, some heads and teachers perceived competition, whether formal or informal. Formal competition arose in the process of bidding for funding:

> It's quite interesting because, although ... in most of the local authorities now there will be a Traveller Education Service, we don't all operate in the same way. When we bid, although there is debate around this issue as to whether or not it is com-petitive bidding, I think it has to be ... although the DfEE insists it isn't. (Interview M)

Informal competition arose from the feeling that Travellers and schools might compare the apparently different levels of outcomes by TESSs and not under-stand the widely varying inputs by LEAs that caused this: 'It puts a sort of pressure on as well, because while other authorities, other services are developing fabulous resources and come up with this shining stuff, we don't have time for that' (Interview N).

The benefits and the occasional drawbacks of teamwork among Traveller educators within their own TESSs could be seen in their relations with heads and teachers in other TESSs. Benefits clearly outweighed drawbacks: having access to the largely informal networks among TESSs in different parts of the country was a source of information and inspiration to many Traveller educators and in some cases made the difference between survival and success or ineffectiveness and failure. The drawbacks related mainly to competition and reflected positioning by external forces, particularly funding providers and Travellers. Certainly a key element of supporting the learning of Traveller students was the systematic sharing of ideas and resources among TESSs.

The opportunities for effective teamwork at the national level that mirrored the relations among TESSs and in individual TESSs were embodied by NATT. In its steady growth over 25 years it developed into a significant voice for Traveller educators and an important site for the implementation and dissemination of innovative practices in educational provision. Thus it helped nurture new Traveller educators and enabled experienced TESS heads and teachers to try out new ideas and respond to the changing policy landscape.

Most respondents who referred to NATT were enthusiastic about its role in enabling them to broaden their professional horizons. As N stated, NATT '... is vital. It's a lifeline'. B called the biennial NATT conference '... the only opportunity we would have to meet people from all over Great Britain'. And J perceived NATT's role as working in concert with relations among TESSs:

> Personally, from meeting with regional people and discussing issues on a regular basis that are going on, and from national training such as the literacy and numeracy strategy, I certainly think staff feel they are exploring the main issues and they're able to talk to other staff about it.

However, NATT could not be all things to all Traveller educators. Sometimes individuals felt that not all their professional learning needs were being met:

> ... conferences with other Traveller educators obviously ... are useful. We have a regional conference once a term; there's a national conference every couple of years; and there's various other meetings. They're useful, but I don't think they really fulfil a [function] when you're talking about professional development. Speaking to people in other authorities I think they've said very similar things. (Interview G)

E had been involved in NATT from the outset so had a historical perspective on both the initial impetus for establishing the organisation and the changes that framed its evolution over time. She reflected on the close link in status between Travellers and Traveller educators:

> ... we had so many examples in the early days which actually caused me to ask people at one of the early conferences, 'What about setting up a national association of teachers of Travellers?'. Because we had so many people working in very poor environments without supervision or support, without the resources. They were experiencing as teachers of Travellers the same rejection by colleagues for

instance, and even by their line management, as the Travellers themselves were experiencing. So the national association – the original idea was that we would decrease the isolation, that we would share good practice.

NATT's development from seeking an antidote to the marginalisation of Traveller educators to striving to exercise national influence over government policy-making was neither automatic nor easy. It reflected the determination and capacity of diverse individuals and groups to share ideas and support and to agitate for a public voice about the circumstances and needs of their students. They were willing to link educational provision with broader and deeper issues of social structure and power that other educators – and some within their own ranks – might find uncomfortable. They have been encouraged and sustained in this by their relations with other Traveller educators within and across TESSs and in NATT.

Implications for practice

Working in Traveller education can be a lonely business. We have discussed the importance of teams and teamwork, but in smaller authorities there might be just one or two teachers working with Traveller families and schools in quite isolated circumstances. Even those working in teams may meet colleagues only once a week. These teachers have none of the daily professional support of colleagues, which can make the best schools into cooperative learning communities. They have no staffroom to go to for respite or informal discussion with other teachers when they are having a troubled day. Sometimes difficult professional judgments have to be made on the spot without backup. So other personal support networks are vital for those working in TESSs.

This was what led to the formation of NATT in 1980, after a national conference. It aimed to provide a mutual support network, discussion forum and professional development opportunities for teachers working with Traveller children and families and it persists more than 25 years later for the same purposes. Organised voluntarily by members, it runs three one-day conferences each year, hosted by TESSs in different parts of the country, where experience can be shared and practice developed from needs assessed on the ground. Teachers of Travellers are engaged in innovative, often pioneering work, and these conferences offer the chance for good practice to be disseminated and problem areas debated. Groups within NATT work on policies and strategies for potential areas of development, such as information and communication technologies, and make formal responses to government consultations. They hold a major national conference every two years and also a resources day, which provides a market place for TESSs to buy and sell culturally specific books, photo packs and other materials they have produced. In the absence of clear government policies for Traveller education, services have worked together to determine the most effective ways to progress. Only in 2003 did government publications (DfES, 2003; Ofsted, 2003) bring together TESS thinking and other research into a model of best practice.

TESSs in most parts of the country also meet regularly in regional groupings to provide professional development. The working conditions and some of the training needs are generally specific for TESS staff, so it is common for such sessions to be generated in-house by a sharing among services. Teachers who are known to have had success in, for instance, secondary transfer and the retention of Traveller children in school beyond the age of 14 will be invited to discuss their strategies with colleagues in the region. Similarly, TESS coordinators meet in regional groups to discuss the issues pertinent to their geographical areas.

Despite many years of competitive bidding for funding, TESSs cooperate a great deal. Partly because of the marginalisation of many teachers and services within their local authorities, they need networks of support and a sense of common purpose. Although TESSs have lately moved closer to other services, such as those offering English as an Additional Language (EAL) support, they are still unique in that their first and basic challenge is to achieve access to school for Traveller children. Since funding for Traveller education projects moved into the larger grant for Vulnerable Children and more recently to the Children's Services Grant, TESSs need more than ever to support one another and to speak with a common voice about the particular needs of Traveller children.

Teachers in neighbouring authorities will inevitably meet some of the same children when working with mobile groups,, especially those whose families follow a regular travelling pattern. This, too, promotes cooperation. These children need as much continuity in provision as possible, but this is not easy to achieve across local authority boundaries. Neighbouring authorities may be run by different political parties and have different priorities and policies concerning Travellers. Budgets, staff numbers, activities and the degree of development of the TESSs will vary from place to place. Traveller parents may be confused and disappointed to find that a certain provision they have come to expect is not maintained when they move a few miles down the road and cross a county boundary and friction can arise among neighbouring TESSs.

Take transport to school as an example. This might be provided in one authority but not another for reasons of funding or policy. Some TESSs will make initial assessments of children at home and gradually introduce them to school, while others never work on sites but only on school premises. Some services can provide on-site support to fairground and circus children who are travelling with distance learning packs; others do not have the staff for such work. Sometimes discussions at NATT or regional meetings dwell on the detail of such day-to-day issues at the expense of the broader picture of the distinct needs of the various travelling communities. But for hard-pressed TESS staff, coping with the numerous demands on their time, it can be difficult to look beyond the immediate challenge.

There are some excellent examples of cooperation among TESSs. In the northeast, the response to the huge gatherings of Showmen for Newcastle Town Moor and Hull Fairs was to provide schools on the fairgrounds for the duration of the fairs, staffed by TESSs from all the neighbouring authorities working together. Another group of TESSs chose not to bid against one another for development funding to produce literacy resources but submitted a joint bid and worked together over several years on a pack of materials to motivate and improve the literacy of teenage Travellers. NATT coordinated a national data gathering exercise on the number and frequency of evictions so they had statistical evidence to demonstrate how much the lack of site provision affected access to education.

During the 1990s European Commission funding for projects to promote educational opportunities for Travellers also facilitated TESSs working with one another and with colleagues in other European countries. The European projects brought a breath of fresh air. Here was a chance to go beyond the confines of a fairly small world in the UK and share experience with others who worked with Traveller groups and had similar challenges but different responses and working circumstances. Teachers were enabled to gain new perspectives on their work over exchange visits, bringing back interesting ideas to try out in their own areas. The opportunities for professional development were significant. Services which could relate the European project work directly to the day-to-day issues within their own localities gained enormously.

However, others found the European projects too far removed from their daily reality, offering little more than extra paperwork for scant return. Other TESSs were too small to devote staff time or energy to such projects. This was a potential source of tension and could increase the sense of marginalisation fclt by the small services, especially if the results of others' participation could not be shared.

The current concern for Gypsy, Roma and Traveller communities expressed by the European Commission and other international bodies helps to keep the issue of Traveller education on the UK agenda.

There is now enormous experience among TESS coordinators and teachers and the relationships among them are increasingly important. Those relationships were often forged initially for personal survival in emotionally exhausting jobs. Now the collective professional voice of TESS teams across the country is needed to keep the attention of policy-makers on the job of ensuring equal educational opportunities for Traveller children.

Part 2:
Traveller Sites

3

Relations with Traveller children

These relations are vital in giving some continuity and stability to young people whose educational lives are so interrupted and who may have had many negative experiences of schooling. Unlike a regular class teacher in a school, who sees a different group each year, the Traveller education teacher often follows the progress of individual children and families – albeit in fragments – throughout their educational lives, and into the next generation.

The teacher-student relationship is the central association in the educational enterprise. Ideally this relationship is dialogical, mutually respectful and attentive to the rights and interests of the other. In practice, it is often fraught with misunderstandings and characterised by power plays – on both sides.

This is partly because the teacher-student relationship is the intersection between two complex networks of associations and two separate systems: school and family. Each system has its own historical origin and development over time, its own aspirations and goals and its own external and internal pressures and tensions. Sometimes these systems of school and family interact harmoniously; at other times their competing demands spill over and have a negative impact on the relations between teachers and their students.

Leaton Gray's (2006) analysis of *Teachers Under Siege* highlights several of these complex interactions. On the one hand, the shift in thinking about teaching from a vocation to a utilitarian exchange of knowledge and skills for public status has tended to erode teachers' autonomy and devalue their contributions (pp155-156). On the other hand, utilisation of technological advances and new forms of social networking by young people lead some of them to question what adults can provide for their education (p156). Teachers are positioned squarely in the centre of these two powerful and mutually enforcing, yet contradictory, forces, with both their authority and their relevance under attack.

Likewise Ellsmore's (2005) interpretation of the four types of charismatic teachers *Carry On, Teachers!* was located directly in the teacher-student relationship while also illustrating these broader social forces and networks. Many teachers appeared domineering, even egocentric, yet all of them made what they variously perceived as their students' immediate and long-term interests the central focus of their actions. There was thus an attitude of 'us together against the others' that forms an important, but by no means the only, dimension of TESS staff members' relations with their Traveller students.

A particular feature of the teacher-student relationship when the students are considered marginalised (Anteliz *et al*, 2006a) is the teacher's ambivalent position as an agent of a system that can potentially perpetuate the sources of that marginalisation. From this perspective, 'us together against the others' might take the form of engaging in recognitive rather than distributive or redistributive social justice, whereby 'the cultural politics of social institutions, such as schools' (Gale and Densmore, 2000, p18) are acknowledged as influencing the life chances of learners and 'difference is differently valued' (p20). This means that teachers working within this framework have to guard constantly against being complicit with the broader sociocultural forces that construct existing inequities and that their relations with their students are vehicles for promoting the latter's lifelong opportunities. As Gale and Densmore (2000) observe: 'Teachers bear such responsibilities towards their students; they and interested others are obligated to think again about the classroom relations they establish and how these might be reworked to better serve their students' interests' (p107).

That only twenty of the 44 students in Derrington and Kendall's (2004) study completed the first three years of secondary schooling illustrates this continuing challenge. While the authors noted that this '... may also reflect an encouraging message when compared with earlier estimates that less than one in five Traveller students accessed school in Key Stage 3' (p173), all of the twenty successful students were settled enough to be tracked for the length of time of the research. This finding reinforces the urgent need for continuing support for Traveller children and the importance of good relationships between the children and TESS staff members in providing that support.

Another example of reworking envisaged by Gale and Densmore (2000) is the importance of recognising that, rather than being blank slates with no substantial pre-existing knowledge, Traveller students, like all learners, bring with them into classrooms and schools rich cultural traditions and robust skills and understandings derived from their respective communities. For instance, Gobbo (2006) noted the considerable experiential knowledge and emotional and social maturity of children of Italian *attrazionisti viaggianti*, the travelling operators of circus and fairground attractions:

> The caring attention with which a young boy measures the area where the attraction will be put up, or steers a big truck so as to park it precisely within the boundary assigned to it, while from the pavement his father points out to him which way to steer, and the alert quickness with which teenagers (boys and girls alike) climb and balance themselves on the metal beams of a rollercoaster dome to spread the plastic top over it, are visible indicators of a successful enculturation that starts when children are very young and, especially at the beginning, does not require the older generation to transmit information or rules verbally. As children are always around the family members, they have multiple opportunities to watch how adults go about putting up (tirar su) and taking down (tirar giu) the attraction and how they solve unforeseen problems concerning it or its means of transportation. (p793)

TESS heads of service and teachers are usually aware of this pre-existing knowledge and it forms part of the foundation of their establishing effective and enduring relations with their Traveller students. Unfortunately schools are not always so cognisant of these skills or of the maturity that Traveller children are accustomed to displaying in their communities. Inevitably this makes the TESS staff members' relations with their Traveller students more complex and means that they might take on the dual role of advocate for the students with schools, and coach or counsellor with the students. Certainly most if not all Traveller educators would concur that establishing respectful and sustainable relations with their students is crucial to maximising learning outcomes.

Several of these themes were evident in our study. Some statements were assertions that might be expected from any educator speaking about learners; others reflected the particular circumstances of working with Travellers.

A number of respondents referred to the kinds of relationship that they aspired to develop, and in some cases succeeded in developing, with their Traveller students. For example, P located her relations with her students at the core of why she remained in such a challenging job and at the centre of what made it so challenging:

It's the children. They are delightful. If I get a bad day – we had one here the other day when one boy ran away ... We have bad days when things happen, where situations evolve, where, if you had had a little bit more hindsight, situations evolve that shouldn't, and then you feel terribly guilty. Those are your low days, and your high days are like when [a Traveller child] picked up those Level 5s. You're so pleased for him; he was absolutely beside himself. The sorrow, his parents didn't really understand it; he did, but they didn't, and to them it wasn't an ultra-relevant thing.

An important element of this teacher's relations with her students was that she had worked in Traveller education long enough to have seen beneficial changes to those students' opportunities and life chances:

... I've seen Traveller children not getting invited to birthday parties when I first started. When you see them going as a normal thing, and when you see children from their school going on the site to children's birthday parties [– those are the high days]. I know it's little things ... One of the boys who is moving up to the high school from one of our other schools is in the town brass band. Ten years ago... I wouldn't have got the free instruments. If they're showing ability for music [here], they get a free instrument and they just pay two pounds a week for the lesson which comes out of my budget ... You just wouldn't have seen Gypsy children in the town band. (Interview P)

This teacher's emphasis on working closely with the Traveller children to find and build on their individual and shared interests and strengths fitted with the statements about the necessity of helping the children to gain confidence and to learn. J identified teaching as a vocation and developing rapport with learners as the central element of that vocation, regardless of the learners' backgrounds:

From a professional point of view, if teaching's a true vocation and you're doing it because that's all you ever wanted to do, then I think you could meet the educational needs of the children, and I think if you see it as a vocation you're more empathetic to children anyway and you're on their wavelength so you get on well with them.

E drew on her long experience in Traveller education to reflect on the previous situation '... where the lack of understanding about their particular experiences had caused people to see the children as failed learners rather than [as] youngsters who hadn't had the opportunity to learn formally'. Consequently she chose to highlight the distinctive character of establishing good working relations with Traveller students:

... [Travelling children are] youngsters who can't rely on whole teaching sessions in order to develop their knowledge or skills or learning, and so we need to give them 'how to learn' strategies so that they're useful skills whether they're in school or out of school.

F explained how this crucial distinction between Traveller children as 'failed learners' as against 'youngsters who hadn't had the opportunity to learn formally' had a direct impact on her pedagogical practice and her relationships with them:

> We are not a learning difficulties or a special needs support service. We're there because they've got needs because they're Travellers. All the time you have to keep sitting down and saying, 'Why are we doing this? Is this child in difficulty because he has a learning difficulty or because he's a Traveller? Or because he is a Traveller with a learning difficulty? Which bits am I trying to support?' So all the time we are working on that.

Two participants in a joint interview drew attention to the importance of being flexible and individualising the pedagogical approach to take account of a particular child's situation at a specific time. They commented on how they had seen Traveller students being taught in schools. One respondent noted:

> It's simple things like the approach to teaching. You get the intelligent young person in who's never been to school before. Instead of starting from what they know and working outwards – in maths, for example, they might have quite good mental maths abilities ... they'll start them at the beginning with one and one, and teach them the actual number. The child might not know what the numbers look like. So that is important. (Interview K)

Her colleague concurred: '... [I]t's the same with reading. They go right down to the beginning and teach them the phonics. The child doesn't need the phonics; the child needs to understand what you're talking about whatever you do' (Interview K).

The first respondent continued the discussion:

> With reading, we always start with making our own books and things like that with the kids' own experiences. But the schools, they seem to see them ... as somebody who can't do it and therefore you start at the beginning like a reception child. They don't see it as somebody who has a lot of experiences already and abilities, just not this one ... They have real problems. They have a system set out of how children are supposed to learn and the order they're supposed to do it, and they want to follow it. They follow it slowly, even though the kid might be like a sponge. (Interview K)

Some respondents took up the point that Traveller students come to school arrayed with a range of experiences and skills that are crucial elements of who they are as people and as learners but that are not necessarily recognised in the school system – sometimes to the detriment of establishing meaningful relations with them. As O noted:

... if they're performers in the circus, they obviously have to put an awful lot more effort into the learning of the business ... They'll be very busy doing that and learning how to deal with it. There's the ongoing performances and practising if you're actually part of a performing family.

In the same vein, the TESS staff member who had at one stage worked as the teacher with a travelling circus recalled the richness of the circus children's informal learning experiences as they taught one another new performance skills:

... one year we had a girl who was determined to learn to walk the wire, so everybody would join in and have a go. So I think there is that sort of cross-fertilisation in ideas. Another year the kids were really into unicycles, and it wasn't just one kid, there were three or four of them, ... so I suppose it depends what the trend is, or whether you've got somebody who can train you in that skill. Another year we had a trampoline around a lot because there was an act on the show, and somebody would say, 'Can I have a go?' Then they'd get into that. So I think circus people are quite good at sharing their skills; they're prepared to help people. (Interview S)

This recollection reflected a deep working knowledge of the students' community and – at least implicitly – a regret that large schooling systems could not easily adopt flexibility in the students' formal education. K observed:

I think with the Travelling pupils it would be a problem getting schools to recognise that a child might be gifted depending on the literacy levels the child had when they came into school. They tend to judge very much on the literacy level and not on the other skills or abilities that the young people have. That's something we're battling against all the time.

R noted the informal skills Traveller children acquired growing up in mobile communities: 'The girls learn a lot of life skills at home because they look after the younger siblings and they are expected to clean out the trailer or the house, while Mum relinquishes those activities as she grows older'.

Some participants referred to individual students with whom they had developed a close rapport or who were especially memorable. For example:

... we've got one little boy that is definitely very bright. He's year four, and you can give him anything to read and he'll be able to read it. You go into the classroom: he has always got his head in a book ... I think when he gets into doing SATS [Standard Assessment Tasks] at Key Stage 2 he'll do very well. But the thing is, will he be allowed to continue into high school? So that's one bright boy we've been able to see with the Gypsy Travellers. (Interview T)

G was less fortunate:

> I must admit it is frustrating when you really seem to get to grips with something. I remember ... I had a girl who had never been to school before [and who] arrived – in the days of the eight to twelve schools I was talking about – in the top year ... so she was 11 or 12 without having any idea of how to read, and saying, 'I haven't been to school'. Yet within a month she was starting to make those first steps, which is incredible. She must have been an incredibly bright girl. I thought really I was getting somewhere, then suddenly within a month she's gone. I never saw her again. Some come and reappear, but some just disappear altogether. That can be very frustrating.

Effective and sustainable teacher-student relations are clearly the cornerstone of successful Traveller education. But as we have seen, good relations are not always easy. Traveller educators have to work hard to establish rapport with students as individuals and make connections with their lifeworlds. And they have to resist any tendency of the educational systems they represent to take over the children's lives or to be seen as threatening or hostile. Students also have to be willing to meet their teachers half way and to be receptive to the kinds of support offered to them. J summed it up: '... you've got to get on well with these pupils'.

Implications for practice

What do you say to a child who refuses to go to a new school because she was bullied and called names in her previous school, whose parents are not keen on school as their own experience of education was negative and to whom you know that the headteacher is reluctant to give a place anyway?

What do you say to a teenage Traveller from a Showman's family who doesn't want to return to school for the winter, after the touring season? He has been treated as an adult, apprenticed to the family business and participating in decision-making all summer, and knows that at school he will be treated like a child. He knows that he will have fallen even further behind his peer group in academic subjects and that he will feel ignorant, even though he sees little relevance in those subjects to the life he will be leading in future on the fairground.

What do you say to a child who says, 'Will I have to give another talk about my life in the circus?' It could be the 20th one that term.

These scenarios will be all too familiar to teachers in TESSs. Dealing with such questions and issues has been at the core of their work. Only a minority of the children have full access to pre-school or nursery education; mobility means continual interruptions to school attendance and maybe frequent changes of school. Depending on their own schooling, or lack of it, parents may not be supportive of formal education. Some schools are hesitant to take in children who might weaken attendance figures or performance levels, despite the strong push for policies of inclusion. The children clearly need support. But who should give it, and what kind of support should it be?

For many years TESS teachers, combining teaching with outreach work to families, were the most significant educational link for Traveller children. They visited homes and talked through the anxieties of the children and parents. In some areas an initial assessment might be carried out on site. The TESS teachers accompanied the children on school visits and followed up with a period of teaching support if necessary. The sight of a familiar face in school reassured the children. In larger TESSs these roles might be separated out among education welfare officers, field workers and support teachers, but many teachers performed a combination of all these tasks and formed close relationships with children and parents over years. Though it was frustrating when children moved on before making real progress, being able to follow some children, *albeit* intermittently, right through primary and secondary school was very satisfying.

There has been ongoing debate about what kind of support is appropriate for TESS teachers to give Traveller children in school. Withdrawing a child or small group from class and giving separate, focused literacy or other support may seem like a good idea for those who are far behind their peer group. But they will miss other learning opportunities while absent from the class and, more importantly, it will confirm that they are different, needing a visiting teacher, and this can hinder their integration into the class. Some TESSs have therefore offered only in-class support to Traveller children. Teachers come into the classroom and work alongside the class teacher, supporting Traveller and non-Traveller children in small mixed groups. But this does not allow the class teacher time to get to know the particular needs of the Traveller children, so some TESS teachers take the whole class on occasion to give the class teacher the chance to make a detailed assessment of the Travellers.

Many Traveller children have been inappropriately placed in the special needs category, when teachers have failed to recognise that they are not dealing with a child with learning difficulties but one who has had little opportunity for formal learning. This is a complex professional judgment to make and needs time and the opportunity for careful observation. Busy class teachers have often relied on TESS staff to help them make these judgments.

Given the large numbers of children in their area and the relatively few staff, or because of policy decisions, other TESSs help only with assessments and differentiation of work for Traveller children in school. The major respon-sibility for the education of each child must lie with the school and the class teacher. Many services therefore give time to the development of teaching and learning resources that reflect the various Traveller cultures. One purpose of such materials is to let Traveller children see their own culture acknow-ledged and give them a familiar context in which to approach school work, but the job is only half done if Traveller children are alone in using these re-sources. Respect for Travellers will not develop unless their lives and attitudes are reflected in materials used by all children as part of the whole school curriculum.

Traveller children and class teachers long depended on the benign interven-tion of TESS teachers, but the balance of responsibility has gradually shifted. For a time the conditions of the DfES grant for Traveller education projects obliged services to concentrate on the access, attendance and achievement of school age children but then developments were encouraged in early years education. Also attention shifted to the 14 to 19 year age group, which led to innovative projects in vocational education for some groups. Such projects, which could involve family apprenticeships, evoked respect for family taught skills and increased motivation among teenage Travellers, who are con-sidered adult at 13 or 14 within their own communities. A vocational curri-culum had more relevance for some teenagers.

TESSs increasingly looked at the educational needs of the whole age range but, as they had few extra resources, priorities had to be reconsidered and working policies redrawn. Traveller education projects were being moved into the mainstream and linking with new government initiatives such as the literacy and numeracy hours and the Connexions service, which seeks to aid access to a range of post-16 educational options. These initiatives could benefit Traveller as well as other students, if access could be secured for them and if mainstream teachers took full responsibility.

New government policies recommend a fundamental shift in emphasis with-in TESSs from supporting children to supporting schools and teachers to fulfil their responsibilities to Traveller children. TESS teachers are to spend more time on curriculum development and giving training to class teachers and teaching assistants than on working with children in school themselves. They are to engage in more extensive discussions with headteachers and gover-nors, assisting with race equality and inclusion policies at both school and local authority level.

This current change of emphasis has several implications for TESS staff. It dovetails with the DfES (2005) new expectation of schools, that they should have personalised learning plans for every child. Traveller children should not be excepted. Targeted support should be given for intervention and catch-up provision for children who have fallen behind in English and Mathematics, and to develop the education of gifted and talented learners. Schools should work closely with other children's services and focus particularly on groups of children who are underachieving, providing parents with better information about their child's progress and helping them to engage in their learning. TESSs are to help schools to meet these new demands with regard to Traveller children.

Many TESS teachers will become teacher trainers and advisers, rather than teachers – welcome professional development for some, but an uncomfortable role for others who do not feel fully prepared. The status of relationships at various levels will change, as we will see, and some close relationships with Traveller children will be lost. It is important that trusting relationships with families that have been built up by TESS teachers, often over many years, are not lost. But these must not stand in the way of direct relationships between Traveller families and schools. It is a difficult balance to find and maintain. Above all, Traveller children have to be empowered to make their own informed decisions. Most TESS heads of service and teachers believe that essentially their jobs are about giving Traveller children the tools to make choices. How that is best done is a continuing exploration and challenge.

4

Relations with Traveller
parents and families

Good relations with parents and extended family are vital. Unless parents trust teachers, they are unlikely to let their children attend school. The demands and expectations of school can conflict with the Traveller idea of education within the family and an apprenticeship approach. Cultural values may differ and be a source of tension, but strong working relationships between parents and teachers can lead to significant achievements by Traveller children and even bring parents back to more formal learning.

Teachers' relations with parents and families are complex and diverse. They range from minimal contact – perhaps the annual parents' evening attended mainly by the parents of academically successful students – to parental involvement, even integration, into school decision-making as school governors. In between are the variegated networks centred on school communities. Active involvement in preschools and early years education is likely to dwindle when children enter secondary school.

We have maintained that teachers are positioned at the intersection between two powerful systems: home and school. So educators who seek to maximise their students' learning outcomes need to understand and establish strong links with students' lifeworlds. This is by no means straightforward: families often have pressured lives and not all parents want direct involvement with their children's schools. Yet the domains of home and school are interdependent and the focus of contemporary educational discourse on networks and partnerships emphasises this interdependence.

Nevertheless, as Weafer (2001) reports about Irish Traveller parents' perceptions of educational provision for their children in the Archdiocese of Dublin:

> While most parents are happy with the primary school system and recognise the improvements that have taken place, there is a sense of uncertainty regarding the ultimate value of education to Travellers. Opinions ranged from the majority who would be satisfied if their children learnt the basics and '*got a good job*' to the minority who see education as the way forward for the next generation of Travellers. Everyone hoped that their children would '*do better for themselves*' but, in the main, they don't know what types of jobs their children could or would receive. Their children are still much more interested in the Traveller economy than in getting a 'regular' job. Uncertainty regarding the future employment prospects and the role of education in this process is heightened by the lack of success some Traveller children have in looking for jobs. Discrimination may be less overt but it is still perceived to occur. (p31; emphasis in original)

Weafer (2001) contrasts this ambivalence with the parents' attitudes towards formal literacy instruction:

> ... a number of parents, particularly those who are involved in local literacy or training initiatives, also spoke of the gap in their own lives: '*I never knew it was so important to read and write. It's only now I know how important it is and how much I lost in life not knowing how to read and write. I hope my children and grandchildren won't be as stupid as me! No-one I know can read or write and we are lost in filling forms and reading letters. Settled people don't understand this.*' Their parents were too 'easy-going' when it came to their education and a transient lifestyle did not fit into the educational system of the time. However, they are hopeful that their grandchildren and children will learn more than they did. (p31; emphasis in original)

Gobbo (2006) recorded the value system that underpinned the approach of Italian *attrazionisti viaggianti* to enculturating their children:

> All *attrazionisti* ... will emphasise values such as self-reliance, independence and autonomy as their own and transmit them to their children through everyday work practice and informal conversation. Thus, adults will not only praise and respect other colleagues (and even the younger *attrazionisti*) for their worthy behaviour but also underline how such values are for instance externalised in the capability to enact multiple practical skills. (p795)

She too (Gobbo, 2006) notes the ambivalence that framed the *attrazionisti viaggianti* families' attitudes towards schools. On the one hand, they recognised the instrumental value of schooling for their children: '... compulsory education is valued because, as ... [one interviewee] said, 'in our sector it means a lot to have an education. [It's necessary] in order to get along with [sedentary] people' (p799). On the other hand, they felt that schools perpetuate stereotyping and prejudice:

Children in school are also mistaken for Gypsies the first time that they attend a classroom and they must often suffer their classmates' unpleasant remarks or wary relations ... the routine contacts with schools can at times be unpleasant because the application forms have pre-printed category descriptions such as 'itinerant', 'nomad' and '*giostrai*' [negative term for *attrazionisti viaggianti*] that makes many of them very upset. [One interviewee] claimed that she never felt insulted by the bureaucratic form and by school secretaries' ignorance and remarked that:

> After all, secretaries didn't know how to describe so correctly. The latter couldn't even imagine that some of us would get very upset ... Secretaries know nothing, they don't know that *giostrai* is a negative label; we do know that it is, but others? (p799)

Similarly, O'Hanlon and Holmes (2004) describe how one Traveller parent who had left school before secondary school was 'very proud' because his eldest child was now attending secondary school, whereas other parents sent their children to school 'only because they had to and not because they really wanted them to attend' (p84). Parents expressed pride in their cultural traditions but were less sure that schools should teach their and settled children about those traditions.

All of this reinforces Kiddle's (2000, p272) powerful plea for 'power-sharing partnerships' between Traveller parents and schools as 'a pre-condition' of greater participation in secondary education, particularly by Gypsy Traveller children. She described how one example of exemplary practice, the Devon Consortium Traveller Education Service's video project, *Between Two Worlds* (Devon Traveller Education Service and Marjon TV, 1993), included training sessions involving fairground parents and class teachers that achieved a shift towards highlighting parental voices. However, establishing this shift on a more generalised basis was a challenge. Kiddle (2000) pointed out that '... a partnership demands power sharing, a mutuality of ground, an exchange between equals' (p271). TESSs can sometimes have difficulty in establishing mutually respectful relations with Traveller parents and families, let alone persuading them to trust what schools can offer their children.

The participants in the study expressed a range of views about their relations with Traveller parents and families. Some were consistent with those of class teachers, while others derived from the Traveller communities' traditional alienation from formal education, thereby creating particular challenges for TESSs in establishing effective and sustainable connections.

A number of interviewees affirmed the centrality of these relations in their work. D stressed '... the crucial nature of the parent-teacher relationship. It's important that that's a cooperative one if it's going to work for the child' and R confirmed the importance that schools 'encourage the families; if they're not getting the support of the parents, then it's really difficult to keep the children in school'.

Relations between TESSs and Traveller parents and families were founded on trust. J summed it up: '... I don't think you get anywhere unless you know the families and they can trust you'. O affirmed this:

> You can't do anything without the parents being keen for you to do it, and to say to the children, 'The teacher's here. Sit down.' And indeed phoning up the teacher to say, 'I'm here, can you come?', which is just wonderful.

However, O also pointed out that 'You've just got to be careful. The relationship with each family's different, and you've got to just learn which you can do that with and which you can't'. She gave an example of what could happen when Traveller parents and families did not trust the teachers:

> Other families who are not particularly interested and see the car coming onto the site, and will just disappear. There's nothing you can do about it. You can't force them to take support if they don't want, and it just leaves you extra time for the other children that actually do want it.

Comprehensive understanding is needed of the multiple and sometimes competing pressures driving the actions and aspirations of Traveller parents and families. Some Traveller communities have more immediate and urgent priorities than ensuring that the children attend school. For instance:

> At the end of the day, my line has always been [that] education has no significance to a woman who hasn't got food in her children's bellies and shoes on their feet. If their most basic needs aren't being addressed, we're not going to get anywhere with schooling. So we have a responsibility to ensure that basic needs are met, to facilitate schooling. That doesn't necessarily mean that we have to do that job ourselves, but we have try and make sure that somebody does. (Interview V)

In the same vein:

> ... we also get involved with health and housing and sometimes the police, situations like that. Because you can't ask a family to consider education or the future of the children when they haven't got a home or they're waiting to be shifted by the police, or there's people ill and they can't access help. All these things come first ... (Interview K)

Another key element of establishing trusting relations with Travellers parents and families is engaging with the ambivalence many Traveller communities feel towards formal schooling, and their fear that it will threaten the continuity and stability of their traditional lifestyle. TESS heads of service and teachers had to negotiate the complex and sometimes risky interface between home and school. E, who had a long experience of working with Travellers, asserted that this was 'particularly' the case:

> ... when you're working with communities who have such a strong tradition of family education and the education has been transferred very skilfully from generation to generation in those communities. They've been independent; they've been self-sufficient ... In fact, that's their first ideology as a community. Suddenly the world changes in a way that is demanding more from them. What are the ways of bringing those traditions together in a way that enables those communities ... to continue to be independent and viable and competitive within the industry that they've chosen? ... It's about changing the whole experience of a community in a way that allows them to keep control and determine their destiny, their future. At the same time, I see it very much as our role to make sure they're familiar with the opportunities, make sure there are no obstacles in the way of taking up those opportunities ...

F discussed communicating the benefits of schooling to the Irish Travellers with whom she worked:

> Maybe that's what we should be doing a lot more is explaining about how they could use what an education will give their children. Not that it will take them away from their culture, but it could be used to reinforce their culture and continue it in a way ... So we do an enormous amount of that transition work and we get them in.

A couple of interviewees mentioned using Parents as Educators courses as particular opportunities to consolidate strong relations with Traveller parents and families. K confirmed that determination was needed, as this goal was certainly not amenable to short-term solutions:

> It's teaching these people to see what they can get from education, put their children through the school and learn as well, and maybe get even more from it. It has to be long-term. It's ... something that might be two or three generations.

Traveller parents and families had to be approached on their home ground and at the same time it was important to make them feel comfortable about entering schools. According to A: 'I think part of a teacher's job anyway is home visits ... It's much more friendly [for parents] than coming into a classroom'. Two participants in a joint interview underscored just how unfriendly many Traveller parents find classrooms and schools:

> Speaker 1. Because most of ... the adults have had very negative experience of school. They've either had very little education themselves, or whatever they've had, it's been unsuccessful, and their parents' memories of school are not happy, in general.

Speaker 2. I've had parent say to me, 'Oh, I can't come to Parents' Evening. They might ask me to write something.' ... They're scared, they're really scared.

Speaker 1. I think it all comes back to what happened to them at school. The teachers perhaps intimidated them, or made them feel small. We've had one [parent] ... We got her along to an open day at a school for one of her youngest ones, and she said it's the first time she'd ever set foot in a school since she was 12. (Interview R)

More broadly, a number of participants articulated the links between such specific actions and the fundamental strategies for engaging Traveller communities in the possibilities and benefits of formal education. They saw TESS's relations with Traveller parents and families as part of a wider and more complex network of associations directed at bringing home and school into greater alignment. As one said: 'It's really important that Travellers are heard, their voices heard, their experiences, as much for their own future generations as for our understanding of these different cultures because they are different' (Interview U). In another example: '... it concerns me that ... real political issues and self-representation issues are not being nurtured, supported or encouraged on the ground. It's a kind of invitation for people to look backwards rather than forwards' (Interview E).

Thus establishing solid and meaningful relations with Traveller parents and families is as complex as developing rapport with their children. Some Travellers see the value of formal education for their communities and welcome TESS heads of service and teachers as sources of knowledge and understanding that would otherwise be closed off to them. Other Travellers see TESSs as emissaries of hostile and threatening systems that treated them badly as children and they are determined that the same fate will not befall their own children. TESS staff members have developed a number of effective strategies for opening and consolidating communication with Traveller parents. However, like any educational strategy, not all are effective with all Traveller communities all the time.

Implications for practice
The relationships that TESS heads of service and teachers build with Traveller parents are crucial. Without trust, Traveller parents are unlikely to allow their children to attend school. The circumstances of every family are unique, but those who face discrimination and prejudice on a daily basis will not easily put their children into a potentially hostile environment. TESS staff, liaising between home and school, have a considerable role to play in easing anxieties on all sides.

Each Gypsy and Traveller group has its distinct reasons for and patterns of mobility. The degree of mobility will have partly determined the parents' access to education and many have had little or no formal schooling at all. Others have had negative experiences. Some regret their own lack of opportunity. Many cope well without literacy skills. So the attitudes to formal education of Traveller parents and families vary widely.

This is particularly noticeable in the early years phase. TESS teachers spend a great deal of time talking about the importance of early years education. If Traveller children start school without pre-school experience, they are already at a disadvantage within their peer group before any interruptions to their schooling take place. There has been some success over the years in this area, with pre-school and nursery projects in many TESSs contributing to measurable improvements in the uptake of such opportunities. Children have been encouraged into community playgroups and nurseries and TESS teachers have given training to pre-school workers. Mobile facilities, such as play buses, have been used, and playboxes, containing materials for educative play, have been created and exchanged using library like systems.

Once trust has been established between parents and TESS staff and then with the primary schools, some parents will make extraordinary efforts to get their children to school. Mothers camped on the side of the road, with no easy sanitary or washing facilities and with an eviction pending, will still get their children to school, neat and tidy and on time. Others travel with a cupboard full of differently coloured sweatshirts, so that whatever the uniform of a new school might be they can ensure that their children fit in, visually at least. Degrees of trust can be recognised. Parents who have found that school is a positive experience for their children may carry one of the school record exchange cards to help with the swift movement of educational records from one school to another. TESSs devised several such schemes, and the DfES later promoted a national system. The subsequent introduction of computerised unique student numbers was intended to make record transfer even easier, though it depends of course on what records exist in the first place for highly mobile students.

Once the trust is there, some parents allow their children to go on trips out of school, though a media scare about an accident in another part of the country may make them rescind that permission. Similarly, a child's bad experience in school, such as being called names or bullied, may lead to the child's withdrawal from education. Relationships are easily damaged and must be constantly maintained.

The time of transfer to secondary school is another key time for TESSs and Traveller parents. 'Time to learn our skills now they can read and write' is a sentiment heard from many Gypsy Traveller parents. On the fairgrounds, children are already in informal apprenticeships to the family business by the time they are 13. Circus children will have been practising their family's skills for years. Some parents are concerned for the moral welfare of their children in secondary schools, and are worried that their own cultural values will be undermined. It is at this time that a good parent-TESS relationship is so important in the interests of the children. Parents and teachers may be making conflicting demands and disagreeing about things such as sex education, and there is a real danger of the children getting mixed messages and being confused.

Despite the gradual rise in transfer rates and attendance at secondary level among Traveller children, there has also been a rise in the number of families who have chosen home education at this stage. The right for parents to arrange education for their children in other settings than school was enshrined in the 1944 Education Act. As long as the education provided is full-time and suitable for the child's age, ability and aptitudes, it is a legal alternative to school.

In the last decade Traveller parents have become more aware of this right and it has been a cause for concern to the TESSs. Although some families are providing adequate educational provision and working with TESS to achieve this, many others are not, simply using the right as a legal loophole to avoid sending their children to secondary school. Monitoring systems in local authorities are generally overstretched and often fail to keep up with mobile families. The concern that many TESSs have about this trend, however, is matched by some understanding of the parents' position. If parents' fears about secondary schools are compounded by a belief that the curriculum has little relevance to them, they are being pragmatic about removing their children and pleased to have a legal way of doing so. The TESS teacher has to move into advocate for education role again, promoting the child's right to choice, and indeed there are examples of Traveller children completing secondary education with academic success and moving onto higher education with the full backing of their parents.

One of the strategies employed by TESSs to aid educational continuity has been the development of distance learning schemes. These were pioneered with fairground Travellers, but also used to support circus families and later other Traveller groups. It seemed particularly appropriate for the Showmen's families, who returned regularly to the same winter base after short stays in a multitude of locations during their travelling season. TESS teachers worked with winter base school staff to provide packs of work which could be done at home or in another school, giving continuity of work to the child. The aim was to provide revision work for known concepts and to cover the essential curriculum elements, which were being taught in the base schools while the Traveller child was away. Over the last twenty years such schemes have become increasingly sophisticated (the technological innovations are discussed in Chapter 10), but the reliance on parent participation remains high.

Parental support is vital if any distance learning system for children is to be successful. Parents must cooperate with schools and TESSs over times that they will be away, methods of exchanging packs of work and when they might return, either at the end of the season or for particular assessments or examinations. They must support their children by providing the tools and a space without distractions for them to do their work. Also they must provide the time to do it without making too many other demands on the children. They must give support and encouragement to the children in actually doing the distance learning work, which is a heavy demand on those who have had very little formal schooling themselves.

TESS heads and teachers recognise how much is expected of parents in the scenario of distance learning and spend time with them, suggesting and discussing realistic and appropriate methods of support. A 'Parents as Educators' course was developed in one region, giving structure to this kind of TESS support to parents and greatly increasing their confidence about managing the distance learning for their children. In another region, research on parents' feelings about distance learning was published in magazine format and then used as training material. In areas where distance learning has been established for many years, some parents have become very experienced in the working of the schemes and have been used as trainers, alongside TESS teachers, for new teachers in winter base schools, who are unfamiliar with the requirements and challenges. Such development, from parents seeking support from teachers to parents giving training to teachers, is one of the signs of progress that TESS staff can recognise over the medium to long term.

The close involvement of parents with their children's distance learning brought some of them back to learning themselves. A number sought help with adult literacy, while others became interested in the opportunities that the new technologies offered. Others asked TESS staff about opportunities for vocational education courses during the periods when they were at their winter bases, and in some areas courses were shaped specifically for the needs and time available of the Travellers. Developments such as these all served to strengthen and extend the relationships between the parents and TESS staff.

The inevitable corollary of developing relationships is that Traveller parents have regularly asked TESS staff about a wide range of issues other than education. Often help was sought to find a launderette, a dentist or a health visitor or a place to stop. The TESS teacher was in some areas the only supportive non-Traveller with whom families had contact. The teachers would come to a site offering to support access to school, while officers from the police or other local government departments would visit with the sole purpose of moving the families on. TESS staff could find themselves in a difficult position. One result of this has been the extension of inter-agency work. If education staff could do outreach work on sites, coping with dogs and other hazards and dealing with the gender issues which might arise when a male teacher came to speak with a Gypsy Traveller mother, there should be no reason why the health authorities and other agencies should not take on their own responsibilities to Traveller groups. In some regions partnership projects were developed, and the recent move to combine parts of Education and Social Services into Children's Services Departments in local authorities should extend this way of working.

Site issues are much more politically sensitive and TESS staff have to tread a careful professional line in the kind of support that they can give to Traveller families. Some teachers have dealt with this by joining a Gypsy Support Group in their local community, which allows them to work on accommodation and race equality issues outside their work time. Others have experienced difficulties in defining the boundaries to their multiple roles. One thing remains clear: the quality of the relationships that TESS staff have with Traveller families will largely determine the effectiveness of the service they provide.

Part 3:
Government and Local Authorities

5

Experiences of government policies

TESSs have had to ride the roller-coaster of changing national government priorities and funding regimes. Without an official national policy for Traveller education for many years, TESSs have individually developed their Services, with all the resulting implications for families travelling between authorities. A series of Ofsted discussion papers and reports has provided some yardsticks and guides for good practice.

This and the next chapter move the discussion from the TESS heads of service and teachers' interactions with Traveller children and their parents and families to another site of influence on their actions and where they also strive to exercise some influence: government and LEAs. In the two previous chapters we argued that TESS staff members are positioned between the two powerful systems and worldviews of home and school. The school system is in turn framed by increasingly frequent and pervasive legislation and policy-making at national and local levels with which TESSs are required to engage and sometimes to implement. In some cases this legislation and policy-making are favourable to Travellers and facilitate their education; in other instances the result, if not the intent, runs counter to Travellers' interests and makes the jobs of TESSs even more difficult.

It is important to acknowledge that this intensification of government impact on the education profession has also occurred in other professions and has significantly influenced the work and identities of teachers in several countries beyond the UK. In terms of the latter point, both the breadth and the depth of this influence were aptly encapsulated by Day *et al* (2006):

Teachers in many countries across the world are experiencing similar government interventions in the form of national teacher education and school curricula, national tests and criteria for measuring the quality of schools, whether through external inspection or a combination of external audit and self-evaluation ... The persisting effect is to erode teachers' autonomy and challenge teachers' individual and collective professional and personal identities. (p172)

Leaton Gray (2006) listed the following seven examples identified by the participants in her study of 'increasing influence of national Government policy' (p81) in the UK as one of the political drivers for change in that work:

- Assessment
- Setting and meeting targets
- League tables
- Policy implementation
- Uniformity of provision
- Private finance initiatives
- Government-led school inspection (pp81-84)

Interestingly these manifestations of government legislation and policy-making do not appear in the films portraying the charismatic teachers analysed by Ellsmore (2005), perhaps because they would be likely to complicate the work of those teachers as they certainly do for real life teachers – and make it more difficult for them to be charismatic and individualistic – again as tends to be the case in real life. A notable exception was the real life Dame Marie Stubbs in the television film *Ahead of the Class* (ITV, 2005), who with her colleagues transformed St George's Roman Catholic comprehensive school in London after the murder of its previous headteacher, Philip Lawrence and in doing so prevented the school's closure.

Binns's (1990) historical overview of the development of TESSs in the UK included the following statement, which predicted the impact of national standardisation in curriculum and encapsulated both the opportunities and the obstacles facing Travellers and Traveller educators as they seek to engage with government policies:

With the incorporation of the National Curriculum classroom teachers will find an extra difficulty in having to cater for pupils who have missed out on large areas of school experience. A sudden influx of numbers of unschooled, unskilled pupils could completely disrupt the teacher's planned progress through the levels of the Key Stages for the class. However, should the Traveller pupil be accepted into school, the National Curriculum could be of great benefit, for the teacher will have to hand a list of progressive stages. The pupil, ideally, will be able to be assessed according to the linear approaches in each Core subject, and given the appropriate teaching experiences to enable the child to begin to catch up with the others. The Attainment Tests could also pose a problem as the Traveller pupils' results could also be seen as reflecting badly upon either the classroom teacher or the school. One suggested solution to this problem is to record the Traveller Pupils' scores along with those scoring similarly regardless of age. (p257)

Conflict over resources and responsibilities between central and local government has a long provenance and was evident, for example, in the uncertainties about how best to engage with the educational needs of children living on English canal boats in the first four decades of the 20th century (Bowen, 2001). That conflict has been accompanied by steadily increasing centralisation of national power, which has fuelled suspicions by some Travellers of the state's ambitions to capture and subdue their difference. As Kiddle (1999) pointed out: 'Government policy pushes onwards reducing the accommodation options other than housing and settlement. It must be difficult for parents to believe that anything other than assimilation is sought' (p64; see also O'Hanlon and Holmes, 2004, pp49-64, for a comprehensive summary of British, European and United Nations legislation and policies pertaining to Travellers). It is these complex and sometimes contradictory experiences of government policies with which TESS heads of service and teachers must engage proactively, strategically and occasionally subversively – to maximise their Traveller students' learning outcomes.

Strong ambivalence was evident in the participants' discussions of government policies. Many discussions focused on the complexities of Traveller education funding, which to some extent tied TESSs's interests to those of the government. Some comments reflected a view that government policies were biased against the interests of Travellers because those interests were seen as threatening the *status quo* and the state power the policies were designed to protect. At the same time, there was acknowledgment that some policies had been implemented with a genuine desire to boost learning, including that of Traveller students, although sometimes those policies were implemented in ways that actually made life more difficult for Travellers and TESSs. Some believed that such policies could function to enforce educational and social change that schools were too reactionary to initiate.

The issue of funding exercised the minds of the respondents. According to D: 'Part of our work is keeping up with all the new initiatives, and ... all the new grants that you can bid for ... It's part of our work for us to try and make the connections'. T reflected on the link between TESSs being beholden to government for three-year funding allocations and also being potentially complicit with government interests and compliant with their policy objectives:

> Because we're funded mostly by the DfEE, obviously we're working with them towards their interests and projects ... so when you're applying for the funding, you've really got to know where they're going before you can decide where you're going.

An experienced TESS head of service elaborated:

> I think ... [the biggest current problem] would be around the government and the DfEE perception of the travelling communities ... [There is a] real need for differentiation at a level of legislation and funding ... So for instance we've really had a history where, despite knowing the different communities that make up the travelling communities, nevertheless the funding and the legislation has largely failed to recognise the needs of the different communities. And I guess there've been some unwritten hierarchies of need within that situation, so that hostility, neglect, prejudice, poverty, disadvantage have gained greater status than the general discussion around the educational needs of children within the different travelling communities, and how and what response we should be making to those different needs ... For instance, historically we've had from time to time the debate about on-site or off-site education provision when we really need to be looking at the different needs across the community and deciding what needs to be mobile, when, what kind of support needs to go in, when, whether it's the curriculum, teacher or the classroom that needs to be mobile and when ... [I]f you're truly serious about bringing communities without a history or a tradition of formal education into the formal process then you really need to be thinking in terms of generational development and not in blocks of three-year funding elements ... A piece of legislation can be introduced, or a new government priority that can actually cause us to put ... [a process] on hold and relook on how that fits in with ... the changed circumstance. (Interview E)

Some interviewees pointed to the positive impact of government policies in bringing about educational and social change that the TESSs would be unable to initiate. As M said: 'The issues that have, as it were, almost dawned on people, has happened very, very recently because of the Ofsted report which highlighted the underachievement of Traveller children yet again'.

Q identified what was wanted in government policy:

> I really feel that there should be a directive from the DfEE to schools to say that they should have a designated person in each school who will take responsibility for Travellers if they come to the school ... [Thus] our job would be easier, life would be better for the Travellers, and I think then we may start to make some progress.

The ambivalence reflected in the analysis of the TESS staff members' experiences of government policies was encapsulated in the respondents' references to the repeal of the 1968 Caravan Sites Act as part of the 1994 Criminal Justice and Public Order Act. Although the Caravan Sites Act had required local authorities to provide sites for nomadic groups, teachers felt that many authorities evaded this responsibility and the powers of central government were used only when legal action was taken:

> Under the '68 Caravan Site Act we had a duty under local authority to provide sites. There was a further carrot of 100 per cent capital expenditure funding for local authorities to provide them. Even so many local authorities ... failed to make any provision, even though you had a Secretary of State who had the powers to direct authorities ... As far as I'm concerned the only time those powers were ever used was when the National Gypsy Council or other organisations actually took the issue to court and there was a direction order from court. (Interview E)

Other local authorities, however, took this legislative responsibility to provide caravan sites seriously:

> To their credit ... [one county] obviously as you can see from the number of sites, invested quite a lot of money in the establishment of authorised stopping places for Travellers ... The idea was a road called the A1 passes through ... [the county] at this point, and this is the beginning of the A1. The concept was, I was told by planners, that there would be a series of these throughout the A1 as you went from North to South, and so Travellers would have a transit site in every county ... However, as the ... [county] planners never fail to tell me, ... [this county] was the only county to build a transit site. (Interview L)

The local authorities that had taken this responsibility seriously were often the ones that adopted a flexible and humane approach to the application of the Criminal Justice and Public Order Act:

> The ... [county] constabulary do not make use of the Criminal Justice and Public Order Act ... They believe that it's more effective to use other more local bylaws. Where the roadside groups aren't moved on is very little to do with what legislation is used and more to do with the fact of who owns the land. Sometimes people cannot find the owner of the land, and Travellers are doing what they've done for centuries, which is exploiting the grey areas that exist in our supposedly well-organised society ... Obviously we have nothing to do with the implementation and the legalities [of the Criminal Justice and Public Order Act]. But we do have a very big issue about those Travellers, ... who are passing through it, haven't got a legal place to stay, and therefore find themselves in various illegal sites. But ... we disregard that. We're not interested in the nature of their residence, we're interested in the mobility of a family, and of course the key to that, the educational experiences of children. (Interview L)

This final point underscored a crucial link between TESSs and government policies: that government policies that made the accommodation situation for Travellers worse had a direct effect on their children's access to school and therefore on the work of the TESSs. In at least some cases, this impact led to informal communication between TESSs and other representatives of local authorities cooperating with one another to try to find ways to support Traveller families while still adhering to the letter of the legislation:

> ... I speak to the man on a regular basis who organises the evictions ... We've only got one official site, and it's only one family at the moment. They're just circulating around the city. He rang me to tell me yesterday morning he'd evicted them from one place, and by the time he got back to his office ... [he called to] tell me where they are now. But he thought they would be evicted again by today ... But we're trying within the systems to get them back into a house. We talk to him, because he keeps us informed, he's the contact with the family. (Interview F)

TESS heads of service and teachers were necessarily adept at identifying and exploiting spaces that were ambivalent and distant from the sources of surveillance of their and other public officials' work. A striking example of this was the Local Government Reorganisation (LGR), elaborated below, which led to the development of new consortia and to changes in the structures of TESSs. While this reorganisation caused considerable stress for smaller TESSs, opportunities also arose for using this legislation to enhance the profile of Travellers and Traveller education and to create new openings for TESSs:

> We've just gone through ... Local Government Reorganisation, and all the divisional structure within the Educational Authority has changed as a result of that. This Equality Education title is new to the new authority ... [M]y line manager has done an enormous amount of tub thumping with respect to Travellers. We did have a situation previously where for a variety of reasons, some of which were political within the authority, it was necessary for Traveller education not to stick its head above the parapet too often, which meant that really we were working in isolation a lot more. But since the reorganisation and since the appointment of a new line manager, that has really changed. He's put Travellers very, very noticeably on the minority culture agenda ... That really is a culture change that has been enormously helpful to us. (Interview V)

Several participants also referred to the crucial interdependence between individual TESSs at the local and regional levels and Her Majesty's Inspectorate (HMI) with responsibility for Traveller education at national level. TESSs strongly commended the collegiality and interest shown by Arthur Ivatts, the Inspector at the time of the interviews. For example: 'He's always supported everyone that's worked in Traveller education' (Interview U); and 'They're looking at expanding the team ... arising from Arthur's reporting. Basically he said it was a superb team, very professional, but is trying to be too many things to too many people. So hopefully we will be streamlining our roles ...' (Interview V). Another said:

> ... we have had a visit last June by Arthur Ivatts, who is an HMI in the field, and he saw what good work was going ... He knows the good intention is there and that we're working well with the families and the schools. (Interview J)

More broadly, there was acknowledgment that feedback from HMI for Traveller education was used to reinforce the validity and value of that practice to the respondents' local authorities:

> Last July I was inspected by the DfEE, by the head man for Travellers, and he referred to my office as 'a drop-in'. He ... [reported] he'd never seen a Traveller education service room on drop-in lines before ... He said I'd excellent relationships, so I am prepared to put up with the inconvenience to me and my staff to ensure that Travellers passing through ... [the authority] know exactly where I am. (Interview P)

Thus the TESS heads of service and teachers' experiences of government policies were complex and ambivalent. This reflected the TESS's often contradictory roles as recipients of government funding and agents of government policy-making. The data demonstrate that these roles sometimes sit uncomfortably with individual TESS staff members, who have had to develop a range of techniques for negotiating around these competing priorities. The minor counternarrative of government policies being deployed as opportunities to initiate much-needed educational and social change and simultaneously to affirm and reinforce the work of TESSs indicated that those techniques sometimes yielded handsome dividends for the efforts of enacting them.

Implications for practice

Governments have always been wary of making opportunities for Gypsy and Traveller children an educational priority, knowing the deep-seated prejudice towards them in settled society. It was not until the late 1960s that the first moves were made towards recognising the needs of these groups. The Caravan Sites Act (1968) finally put a legal duty on local authorities to provide sites for those of a nomadic habit of life, though with no time limit, and the Plowden Report (DES, 1967) brought the scandal of the Gypsy Travellers' lack of access to formal education to national attention. Yet during the 1970s only slight progress was made. It gradually became known that the government 'No Area Pool' could be used to claim retrospective funding for extra expenditure incurred by local authorities in supporting Traveller access to school. Every authority had to contribute to this central fund and then individual authorities could claim back money spent on mobile families, who were not the direct responsibility of any one area. One hundred per cent could be claimed back from the 'Pool' and this enabled the earliest Traveller Education Services to begin. There was no national policy saying what provision should be made, so individual LEAs made their own decisions and Traveller teachers struggled in isolation to find the best way of working. At that time a biennial conference organised by HMI provided the only national networking opportunity.

The funding arrangements changed with the introduction of Specific Grants, which lasted until 2002, and ring-fenced money for Traveller Education projects. There were advantages and disadvantages to the new grants. Central government no longer provided all the money but only 75 per cent and later only 65 per cent. The rest had to come from the local authority and so local political priorities came into play. LEAs had to bid for the Specific Grants and there was never enough in the national pot to meet all requests. So authorities had to bid against one another and there was very little coherence in the development of Traveller services. Also, the grant was offered for only three years at a time, with an annual review, so there was no certainty of continuing funding from year to year. This made long-term planning and retention of staff difficult and the anticipation of and response to the changing educational climate have been constant issues for TESS heads of service. But at least specific funding existed and HMI with responsibility for Traveller education encouraged LEAs to make provision through inspections.

Though there was no national policy, the Department for Education set parameters on how the money could be spent and later targets were introduced. Projects were to support families and schools, enabling Traveller children to have equal educational opportunities to other children. At one stage the conditions of the grant focused all support on school-aged children and so to some extent prescribed local TESS policy. Any virement of grant money desired by a TESS had to be negotiated with the government department. Later a national focus on early years work and a rethink of the whole 14-19 curriculum enabled projects to engage with a wider age range and to work in the context of family education.

Some of the educational priorities of national government have been supportive of Traveller groups even though the policies were not designed with them in mind. The national curriculum and the literacy and numeracy strategies have provided a similar structure within every school, which should, in theory at least, make it easier to move from one school to another. Small group work and targeted support within these strategies can be very helpful to Traveller children. The government's desire to raise the attainment of certain underachieving ethnic minority groups has brought further attention to the needs of Traveller children, though the government research which highlighted this underachievement (Blair *et al*, 1998; Gillborn and Gipps, 1996; Ofsted, 1999) included Gypsy Travellers only marginally. Similarly, the government's inclusion strategy seeks to bring all children into the main-stream, whatever their special needs and circumstances. The task for TESS staff has been to keep up with all the policy developments and to make the connections to their own work, trying to ensure that the needs of Traveller groups are included within all the new initiatives.

Substantial progress in access and attendance at primary school level was made during the 1990s, but the work of TESSs was hindered by two major government changes. In 1994, as part of the Criminal Justice and Public Order Act, the Caravan Sites Act of 1968 was repealed. This meant that there was no longer a duty on local authorities to provide sites for Gypsies and other Travellers, even though almost a third of mobile families still had no legal stopping place. Inevitably the effect was felt in the education sector, and this continues to the present day. Without secure accommodation, regular school attendance is hard to achieve.

The second change was that of LGR, which was occurring in various parts of the country throughout the 1990s. Local authority boundaries were redrawn and new authorities created in a major upheaval of local government. Some of the geographical areas covered by TESSs were now split into several dif-ferent authorities. The new authorities had to decide whether to create a series of smaller, probably unsustainable services or else to enter into consor-tium arrangements with neighbouring authorities to maintain their work with Traveller families. Each area made its own decision, so once again the work of TESSs was denied national coherence. Small services became more isolated, while the heads of TESSs in consortium arrangements had to cope with being accountable to anything between three and twelve separate sets of officers in their local authorities and to deal with all the attendant paperwork.

The new millennium brought further changes with the passage of the Chil-dren Act (HMSO, 2004), which detailed five desired outcomes for children: that they should be healthy; stay safe; enjoy and achieve; make a positive contribution; and achieve economic well-being. To attain these outcomes local authority departments dealing with children were to be reorganised into multidisciplinary Children's Services departments. TESS funding had already changed when the specific grants were moved into a grant supporting all 'Vulnerable Children' and now this grant itself would become part of an overarching Children's Services Grant. TESSs have long worked in horizontal structures, developing inter-agency work and being part of multi-agency forums, so they are well-equipped to meet these new demands. However, the funding for Traveller education projects is no longer ring-fenced and there is a danger that the particular needs and circumstances of Traveller children will be overlooked when treated as part of a bigger picture.

The small numbers of Traveller children whose parents have officially registered their identities in school exacerbates this danger. Schools make an annual return of student numbers to central government on a form (PLASC) which lists ethnic categories. Since 2001 this return has included a category for Gypsy/Roma and Traveller of Irish heritage, but many parents have chosen not to identify their children officially for fear of discrimination. Although TESS staff are aware of all the Traveller children in and out of school in their areas, only a proportion of them are seen in the official figures.

TESSs can lose out because much of the education money from the Children's Services Grant is paid directly to schools, which can then buy back the services of specialist support they require. While this may work efficiently for the services that deal exclusively with children in school, many Traveller children, particularly at secondary level, are still not registered at school at all. Account needs to be taken of all the important outreach and support work undertaken by TESSs, together with the increasing expectations for staff to develop their training and advisory roles in schools and elsewhere.

After 30 years, TESSs have a great deal of experience of dealing with change and the demands of government. They have been aided by strong personal support from the officers in the small Traveller team within the DfES. Models of best practice have been established through extensive networking and a series of HMI and Ofsted discussion papers and reports. Yet, instead of being in the position to discuss national strategies for the specific needs of the distinct Traveller groups with government, they are still fighting for Traveller children's basic rights to formal education.

6

Experiences of Local
Authority policies

TESSs have had to change over the years in response to local and national priorities. Positive relations with senior management in local authorities are crucial to prevent the marginalisation of TESSs within the system. The policies and practice of different departments within a local authority regarding Travellers may conflict with and undermine one another. However, developmental inter-agency work has often been constructive and effective.

We turn in this chapter from the national legislative and policy-making scene to local authorities. Although they differ in terms of history and structure, they significantly influence the work of TESSs and introduce complex dimensions to it. They too create opportunities for TESSs to develop strong and effective working partnerships with other government agencies in ways that enhance their capacity to support the learning of Traveller children.

In the previous chapter we noted Leaton Gray's (2006) synthesis of seven examples identified by her study of 'increasing influence of national Government policy' (p81) as a key political driver affecting the character of their work. Her participants identified the second political driver as 'diminishing influence of local government and LEAs' (p86). Leaton Gray linked this identification with such developments as 'the introduction of Grant Maintained schools in the aftermath of the 1988 Education Reform Act' (p86) and 'the government requirement that some local authorities outsource their services to private companies' (p87). One consequence of this perceived shift was that, as local authorities were seen as exercising decreased power over education, Leaton Gray's participants believed that, while 'Ofsted ... was perceived primarily as a threat ... the LEA was perceived as a type of professional partner' (p87).

Day *et al* (2006) analysed the diminution in the influence of local authorities in terms of 'a larger ideological debate on the costs, management and performance of the public services in general' and specifically in England in terms of education 'as a public service', functioning as

> ... the test bed for a raft of radical reforms from the mid-1970s which were born of political 'new right' ideology and economic pragmatism and a deep distrust of teachers and of public education itself. These reforms challenged the post-Second World War monopoly which professionals in education, health and social services had held. (p171)

While all reforms have an ideological dimension, one theme of this chapter is the increased difficulty for TESS heads of service and teachers in enacting their roles because the other educators and professionals with whom they interact also have difficulties. But such difficulties also create heightened opportunities for cooperation and partnership. Day and his colleagues (2006) maintained that, despite their reduced direct power, local authorities now have greater educational responsibility:

> Teachers will need support at the LEA, school and department level if their enthusiasm, energy, skills and effectiveness are to be sustained throughout their career and life phases so they are able to grapple with the emotional, intellectual and social demands of being a teacher in times of social and educational change. (p190)

Local authorities have varied widely in their understandings of the issues entailed in Traveller education and their preparedness to engage with those issues and to assist TESSs to perform their work in optimum conditions. Binns's (1990) account of the evolution of TESs, for example, shows that some LEAs 'resisted the urge to provide schooling ... [and] pointed out to the DES that in none of the Education Acts was there any obligation to fund education for pupils not living in their area' (p256). This prompted the circulation of 'DES Circular 1/81 and Education Act 1981 which emphasises that each authority's duty extends to all children residing in their area, whether permanently or temporary, including Traveller children' (p256).

Likewise Derrington and Kendall (2004) reported 'wide variation in practice in terms of TES roles and responsibilities' (p69) – so did this study. This variation reflected the historical differences across local authorities and counties in the provision of educational and social services; the differences in the size of the local authorities and the TESSs; diverse opportunities for responding to the changes in Traveller education funding noted above; and ideologically framed conflict between different levels of government spilling over into decisions about staffing and resourcing for individual Services (see O'Hanlon and Holmes, 2004, pp117-124 for one LEA's perspective).

The few references in the literature to relations between TESSs and LEAs reinforce how essential it was for them to be mutually respectful and responsive. For example: 'The support of the TESS by senior LEA officers, including the Director of Education, influences the effectiveness of the service's work in schools' (Bhopal *et al*, 2000, p60). Mott's (2000) research into the role of LEAs in providing education for refugees and asylum seekers encapsulates the responsibilities for Traveller education: 'LEAs were clearly aware of the need at authority level for better planning, improved co-ordination, enhanced networking and partnership, improved translation and interpreter provision and improved support for schools' (p17).

The literature again shows the complex web of interactions and networks framing the work of TESS heads of service and teachers. In many cases their relations with LEAs extend over decades and benefit from the strength of longstanding professional relationships with other service providers and authority policy-makers. By contrast, the national alterations to funding and organisation have tested relationships and required new ones in response to rapidly changing central and local government. This chapter explores some of the ways in which the participants in the research responded to those challenges and the strategies that they deployed to achieve productive and sustainable relations with LEAs.

The data examined for this chapter revealed considerable complexity and ambivalence in TESSs's relations with LEAs. Here too we see poles of complexity and ambivalence. Some TESS staff members felt that they were dealing with uncomprehending and unhelpful local authorities which tolerated their presence under sufferance. Others believed that their authorities, or at least some individuals within them, genuinely appreciated their work and were committed to transforming Traveller education. The complicated and sometimes stressful requirements of inter-agency work were located between these poles.

With reference to uncomprehending and unhelpful local authorities, several participants in the research identified particular difficulties. One set of difficulties centred on the contradictory aspirations and actions of TESSs and other agencies within authorities, particularly in relation to evicting Travellers. As A noted: '... you have us fighting to get children into school [and] you have a certain department of the authority fighting to move them off. We're both paid by the same people'. K stated:

> We have picked up the responsibility of the LEAs' responsibility to assess educational need; that's something we do for the authority within official sites. But the authority doesn't always wait for the report back before they decide to move ... [Travellers on those sites]. We've put quite a bit of time into finding school places, but the families are moved off before any of that happens. So it's an exercise we go through, and then we write a letter of complaint because they didn't wait, then this goes on. This is just part of the process; you just work with it.

N evoked an image of competitive and even chaotic bureaucracy characterising TESS-LEA relations:

> We've now got six groups of people to deal with, and sometimes it's the planning department which effects the evictions, sometimes it's environmental health, but it can be the highways part of an administration that's done that, so it's very complicated. Sometimes it's the Highways Act, sometimes it's local government bylaws and sometimes it's the Criminal Justice and Public Order Act ... We've got people now who are doing this job who have never really had to do it before, and they feel daunted by it. I must say I think that, universally across the ... authorities [from which the TESS was constituted], the elected members would take the view that they would expect the apportioned officers to be getting rid of Gypsies as quickly as possible from the area, because you don't win votes by having Gypsies in the area. So the pressure is on to move them on, not to do what I would call a rigorous or fair assessment, not to see how a site could be tolerated.

D identified contradictory pressures and actions:

> So it really is for the local authorities to come to grips with the site provision, and the central government, because you are getting a much more difficult situation for a lot of families. A lot of families are going abroad (New Travellers) much more, and it's quite interesting that Travellers here have to go abroad to escape from that kind of harassment on the side of the road, whereas from Eastern Europe families are coming here, thinking it's going to be better.

The contradictory aspirations and actions sometimes provoked competition between TESSs and other agencies for scarce funds and other LEA resources:

> I think as other services have been developed we've been top sliced. We've have money taken away from us to provide for those services, but equally our authority has had to make cuts. So when I took over as Acting Head of Service, four years ago now – I've only just twelve months ago been made permanent Head of Service, but four years [later] we had to suffer cuts again, so we were down to seven

teachers, plus me, 1.5 education welfare officers and some admin[istrative] support. That was it. But we have more pupils than we've ever had before, so in this last round of the bid I've actually asked for more staffing. (Interview Q)

There were instances where respondents used internal competition within local authorities to put pressure on agencies they considered were operating in ways antithetical to the work of the TESSs:

One thing that happened in our favour, we asked about costings. If the Gypsies parked on council land, the cost of bringing a bailiff's team out was sent to that department. If they parked on a school, the cost of sending the bailiffs was sent to the Education Department. They all started to get a bit miffed with these bills, so I've noticed over the past year we haven't had the bailiffs out quite so many times. So really it's one of those things of sit[ting] tight, and we've had a quiet winter with the bailiffs. (Interview P)

At interpersonal level, some interviewees encountered what they considered racist attitudes from people working within other agencies in the same local authority:

That still goes on to quite a great extent ... We had a newly appointed village policeman, community policeman. He has a Gypsy site on his patch. Most of the children from that site go to the local little primary school; in fact, 50 per cent of the children on roll are Gypsy Travellers. He turned up to introduce himself at the school, and over a cup of tea was coming out with all sorts of stereotypical comments about Gypsies. When I arranged to go and see him to have a long chat about our respective roles and how we should both work together, to put it politely, he had done all the police training, and yet still was coming out with this racist attitude towards Gypsies. He said they had never been mentioned in all his training. (Interview H)

This experience was echoed by I:

I think the biggest challenge probably is to convince people at policy level, because I've done some training with members, and I was surprised at the racism at that level. You do something on culture to elected councillors, and they're just concerned with evictions and 'Why can't we get rid of them all?' They're the people ultimately in our system that run the show – county councillors are the bosses really – and I perhaps a bit naïvely didn't expect that kind of response. I've got to find some way I think of carrying that forward.

However, several participants spoke enthusiastically about the effective partnerships that they have developed with individuals in other agencies and in their LEAs, and they stressed the positive impact on their work with Traveller children and their families. TESS staff saw it like this:

... if you're going to move forward as a service, you have to (I was going to say infiltrate) be involved with the other agencies and work closely with them, because it isn't just education as just a package on its own. (Interview Q)

E acknowledged the competing cultures of and pressures on the various agencies, including TESSs, and outlined an approach to working cooperatively rather than competitively:

That was when we set about actually deciding – not on an ad hoc basis, but we would actually develop an inter-agency strategy of building networks where we actually sat down together and talked about the case studies, for instance, and what the implications were for education, for health, for environmental health, for accommodation, for planning, for instance. And then looking at how together we could build shared agendas, given that all of those organisations have different cultures [and] different structures that constrain them in some ways. For instance, doing our job might be frustrating for someone else paid by the same authority but [who] actually had the role of moving families on. It was about how we could work together in a mutually supportive way without interfering with each other's work but clearly with an agenda of informing each other's work and looking at how our respective responsibilities could begin to make sense.

J gave an example of inter-agency communication and cooperation:

So again it comes back to my line manager and the director being supportive. I think they know there are training issues, so we link in with lots of other services like the special needs service. Recently there was a conference on hyperactivity disorder, Attention Deficit Syndrome, so our staff were invited to go on that as well. So there's many issues that lots of the peripatetic services make use of each other.

M provided other examples of effective inter-agency partnerships in operation:

... there is actually an official Traveller liaison group which is an inter-agency group, involving people from county, environmental services, planning, the police, social services, also education, health and so on. There's an official link which was actually set up by a predecessor in this service and which I am being encouraged to reorganise by some other members of the group, which we are thinking about. Also we have obviously contact between the different agencies ... The whole issue about inter-agency consultation and negotiation. We are certainly involved in this county, which we are carrying on. Some of the agencies we've been looking very closely at setting up some kind of a protocol, for how we will consult with each other and other issues. It does work, and certainly we have quite a good relationship, most of the time now.

Two other participants articulated what many TESS staff members would see as the desired outcome of a 'good relationship' and inter-agency collaboration. According to V: 'Hopefully that will get easier as the tub is thumped and the training happens and other services increasingly take responsibility for their area of the work'. A contrasted the earlier focus on working alone with the necessity now of engaging simultaneously on multiple fronts with other agencies:

> But largely Traveller education is something that does, to a certain extent, plough its own furrow. By the same token, we're also very, very anxious to include other people in our work. We have inter-agency days ... Once we did work essentially alone; [now] we are educating other agencies as well very much into what we are trying to do.

The two poles of TESS-LEA relations analysed here create additional complexities and pressures in the work of TESS heads of service and teachers. The multiple fronts on which they must conduct their work, even within one authority, increase the potential for misunderstanding or even downright obstruction. Some TESS staff members felt they were being distracted from their real responsibility of working with Traveller children. But those multiple fronts and the ambivalent spaces around them offer possible openings for new partnerships and new ways of working that could sometimes navigate around obstacles and achieve previously unfeasible outcomes. Negotiating effective pathways within the spectrum is a skill Traveller educators require if they are to maximise their students' learning outcomes.

Implications for practice

The discussion in this chapter follows from the last. Local government must mediate policies and priorities set at national level before they are put into action by the front-line services. This is seldom straightforward because of tensions between the central and the local, be it over budgets, politics, practice or power. So TESS heads of service also need good relationships with their line managers and local government officers. The political sensitivities around Gypsy and Traveller issues are most clearly felt at local level.

The most acute concern is accommodation, dealing with unauthorised camping, carrying out evictions and planning for new official sites. Local authority officers know from experience that there will be enormous opposition from local residents to any suggestion of a new official site being located in their area and that pursuing planning applications will be a long and unpopular process. They also know that local residents show little tolerance for any unauthorised campsite in their neighbourhood. They are caught in a double bind and spend fruitless hours and much expense strugg ling to reconcile the wishes of the local electorate with the accommodation needs of Travellers.

The unresolved issue of the shortfall in official site places means that unauthorised camping persists. And this directly affects TESS staff, who seek to achieve optimal continuity in education for Traveller children. Too often the TESS is in conflict with local authority officers from Highways, Planning or Environmental Health Departments over school access or swift eviction. The involvement of the police in cases of unauthorised camping further complicates matters. Opposing policies within separate local authority departments, where the work of one undermines the work of another, are known to be wasteful, expensive and intolerable. Yet satisfactory solutions are hard to find, and have to be sought at the highest level of local government. Some interdepartmental forums have emerged and there is a now a greater understanding of the issues, but progress is slow. TESS coordinators, conducting training for senior council officers and elected members, still experience racist attitudes.

Sites can also be an issue for the circuses and fairgrounds. In some areas animal rights activists have campaigned and had circuses with animals banned. Building developments in town and city centres may remove traditional fairground sites. Any changes to travelling patterns provoked by local political decisions will affect the educational provision planned by TESSs.

On the other hand, relationships with some local government departments and agencies have proved extremely constructive and beneficial. Education departments have been the pioneers in seeking social justice for Gypsies and Travellers. In the early days of TESSs, their staff were likely to be the only positive contact that Traveller groups had with officialdom so TESS workers were asked for support with a range of issues beyond education. TESS practice has moved over the years from doing the work of other agencies themselves, to referring Travellers to other agencies, to instigating inter-agency working and setting up joint projects to plan coherent provision, and then to encouraging other providers such as the health service to take responsibility for planning their own provision.

Not every service has moved right along this continuum. There are variations across the country depending on the particular situation of the TESS. Where the entire Traveller education provision rests with a senior officer with paper responsibility at county hall and a lone worker trying to cope on the front line, such development is slow. However, links with early years, library, youth and community, and Connexions services have spawned all kinds of exciting projects, bringing local facilities within easier reach of travelling groups.

Joint working with health authorities is infinitely more complex as structures and procedures are so different. And as health and education have been subject to a series of restructures, progress towards coherent provision has been difficult to maintain. Nevertheless, constructive relationships have been built up on the ground between TESS staff and local health visitors, district nurses and midwives.

More sensitive are the relationships between TESS and social services, as many Travellers are suspicious of social workers as 'the people who can take your children away'. TESS staff spend a great deal of time establishing trust with the families with whom they work and do not welcome close association with the social services department. However, the recent meshing of aspects of education and social services into Children's Services Departments should create new opportunities for working partnerships.

The 1990s, when some TESSs found themselves in newly formed consortium arrangements as a result of LGR, were a challenging time for maintaining relationships with other local government officers. Although the logic for creating joint arrangements for dealing with mobile groups among newly formed authorities was clear, many of the new authorities wanted to establish their own identities and did not necessarily want to follow the same policies as their neighbours, especially if a different political group was in power. Establishing an effective consortium called on all the diplomatic and negotiating skills of the TESS heads of service. They needed to be effective managers of paper as well as people, now that their accountability was to several masters and they were subject to the full range of assessments and inspections in each of their consortium authorities.

LGR saw a restructuring across all departments with consequent changes in staff, roles and responsibilities at every level. TESS staff had to get to know a whole range of new colleagues, rebuild their local networks and plan new awareness training. Some TESSs carried out link audits to enable their staff to identify the key link personnel in other departments in their respective areas. It was a time of great confusion, but also presented opportunities to spread awareness and understanding of Traveller issues.

Over the last decade, the arrival of Roma families in England from Eastern Europe has brought a new dimension into the work of some TESSs. It is ironic that when Gypsy and New Travellers were leaving the country to escape the harassment they encountered here following the 1994 Criminal Justice and Public Order Act, the Roma were arriving, hoping to escape from the hostility and prejudice they encountered in their own countries. Roma refugees and asylum seekers sparked much media attention, a great deal of it negative, and presented local authorities with new issues and challenges for the education of the public.

TESS staff now had new local relationships to make, with refugee workers and staff from the EAL Services. In some areas completely new projects and teams were created to work with the refugee groups; in others *ad hoc* and not always satisfactory joint working practices were developed. There were sometimes tensions about which services should take the lead responsibility in working with the Roma families and disputes over appropriate practice. In local authorities which housed detention centres for asylum seekers there was even debate about whether education would be provided in the centres at all.

The large-scale movement of people, as refugees, asylum seekers or economic migrants, has become a major issue for all European countries. This keeps Roma, Gypsy and Traveller issues on the international agenda and European institutions expect national governments to demonstrate progress at least in planning for social justice. At the local level, the performance of local authorities is currently inspected through a Joint Area Review. Provision for Traveller groups features as one element in the inspection process, in which authorities must show competence. So, despite the many and diverse claims on the local authority budget, the maintenance of an effective TESS remains essential.

Part 4:
Schools

7

Relations with headteachers

The attitudes and personalities of headteachers create the ethos of their schools. How they react to Travellers coming in and the relations TESS staff have with them are vital to the work of the TESS. Mutual understanding of roles and responsibilities must be developed to avoid tensions or confusion.

This chapter focuses on headteachers and the next on teachers. Relations with both are fundamental elements of the complex and multiple factors framing the teaching of Traveller children.

The extensive and continually expanding literature on school leaders and leadership parallels and illustrates the increasing complexities and demands associated with school leadership positions, particularly headteachers. As schools have been required by legislators and policy-makers to take on more differentiated educational and sociocultural responsibilities, so too have headteachers had to enhance their skill sets and to meet a heightened list of accountabilities and targets.

Doyle and Smith (2001) provided a useful overview of the ebbs and flows in the educational leadership literature by arguing that 'there have been four main 'generations' of theory:

- trait theories
- behavioural theories
- contingency theories
- transformational theories'.

The headteachers with whom the participants in this study interacted were likely to exhibit – or aspire to exhibit – one or more of these approaches to leadership and so did the TESS heads of service and teachers in the study.

Despite the shifts in thinking evident in these democratic conceptualisations of leadership in school settings, the relationship between the person exercising formal or informal leadership and the culturally specific contexts in which that leadership is enacted is key. The political dimension of headteachers' work remains significant. But there are tensions, as Foster (1989) describes:

> In many ways the concept of leadership has been chewed up and swallowed down by the needs of modern managerial theory. The idea of leadership as a transforming practice, as an empowerment of followers, and as a vehicle for social change has been taken, adapted and co-opted by managerial writers so that now leadership appears as a way of improving organizations, not of transforming our world. What essentially has happened is that the language of leadership has been translated into the needs of bureaucracy. (p45)

Some Traveller education researchers have found that headteachers' attitudes towards Travellers strongly affect their learning outcomes. O'Hanlon and Holmes (2004) noted that in schools with little experience of teaching Traveller students the headteachers '… admitted that Traveller culture was not reflected in their schools but most were prepared to consider its inclusion' (p79). One headteacher spoke about Travellers 'fitting in and not being able to pick them out' (p78). Examining two headteachers' views about school policies, ethnicity, resources, self-esteem and the role of TESSs, these authors found that '… in spite of having Traveller children on roll these two schools are yet to become inclusive schools, that fully reflect their multicultural intake' (p97).

Headteachers' attitudes towards Travellers were echoed in their views of TESSs, which ranged from friendly and welcoming to hostile and unhelpful. Derrington and Kendall (2004) found competing assumptions about the responsibilities for discharging the work associated with teaching Traveller children. The headteachers generally expected TESSs to take on most of that work and even direct teaching, whereas TESS staff saw their role as supporting Traveller children and class teachers. Miscommunication and misunderstanding arose over issues such as monitoring Traveller students' school attendance, withdrawing them from mainstream classes and maintaining communication with Traveller parents. 'Most conflict arose in the TES-school relationship when TES staff challenged school actions, for example, sanctions imposed on Traveller students' (p85). As Derrington and Kendall noted, this conflict reflected the deep divergence in worldviews about the character and purpose of schooling, with TESSs seeing themselves as 'cultural mediators' (p85) and as advocates for Travellers against the more powerful and genera-lised concerns of schools and headteachers.

Other headteachers worked to establish a welcoming climate for Traveller students (Blaney, 2005), and one spoke in a way most Traveller educators would welcome, saying:

> It is very evident that the school benefits from the presence of our Travellers. For example their morality and cleanliness have caused many non-Travellers to question their own prejudices; their family loyalty and respect for their parents and extended family are an example to their non-Traveller peers; they provide cultural diversity in an otherwise homogen[e]ous community. Furthermore the learning support and pastoral care of Travellers at Chalvedon [Comprehensive School in Basildon, Essex] have helped our teachers to appreciate that all pupils are individuals with needs. Our Travellers have been integrated into the school without compromise to their identity; as a result the school has gained. (p113)

Despite the importance of headteacher-TESS relations in the work and identities of TESS heads of service and teachers, they are not always har-monious. Given the growing complexity and increased accountability of headteachers, some might see Traveller education as yet another pressure. But assigning as much as possible to TESSs is unlikely to lead to positive learning outcomes for Traveller students. The most advantageous head-teacher-TESS relations are based on mutual respect and trust and on a realis-tic assessment of the roles of each.

A number of participants in the study commented on the personal dimen-sion of their relations with headteachers and how they saw Travellers and the work of TESSs. For I access to headteachers was generally all he required:

> As a team leader I've found that if I want to speak to the head I can speak to the head. I don't insist on always speaking to the head because perhaps sometimes the information you want you can get better from [someone else].

But F felt that her interactions with headteachers were sometimes stressful and had to be managed carefully:

> ... I found it was really hard to negotiate with headteachers [and] that you had to be really firm. Because headteachers want you to do what they want you to do. You have a responsibility for Traveller children and the two are not always matched. I found that there were certain headteachers who I had to be really strong with. I was never told I had to work under the direction of any headteachers ... but there was a limit to what you could do.

Certain interviewees perceived that some headteachers were unaware and hence culturally insensitive to Travellers' experiences. G stated:

> ... we still find sometimes, when you ring a headteacher and ask them to have a new Traveller pupil, you can almost hear ... the cogs going round, 'Travellers, Gypsies. No, sorry, we're full' ... It's largely ignorance. People just don't meet Travellers in the normal course of events.

J recalled:

> I have a very sad story to tell. At a meeting I was at not long after I'd taken over the job where some headteachers were and I had taken some parents along, the headteacher said to me, 'Oh, I had a family who should have come, but I believe they're unreliable'. And he used the term 'tinker' and I don't think he realised how offensive it was.

She also made a point about competing expectations between TESSs and schools about the in-service training that Traveller educators should provide to schools:

> I think it showed me the need for training on two levels really. [One is] raising awareness with a lot of people who are ignorant just because they haven't had experience of this culture. But ... it's all right talking about cultures and celebrations and festivals but that's only scratching the surface. Somebody said to me recently, 'The saris and samosas sort of training' (see also O'Hanlon and Holmes, 2004, p96). I think what I really want to work with mainstream staff about are curriculum issues and how we can help these pupils access the curriculum at their level ...

The statement that 'headteachers want you to do what they want you to do' (Interview F) resonated with the discussion in the literature of differences of view between headteachers and TESSs about the respective and shared responsibilities of TESSs and schools. I articulated how he resisted the view that TESSs were primarily responsible for teaching Traveller students: 'I always emphasise that they're not our children ... It's more than the semantics of the thing. I think it's important that the schools feel that the children are theirs really, and we're there in a supportive background'. But H echoed the headteacher cited by Blaney (2005):

> I think it's back to the 'knowledge is understanding' argument again. We certainly find when the children go into school ... all our Traveller children – if they're welcomed, if their culture is respected, I think that's the important thing, then we have no problems in schools where that goes on.

Given the potential for miscommunication and disagreement between headteachers and TESSs about the responsibilities for teaching Traveller students, negotiating and confirming service level agreements were an important part of the work of TESS heads of service. J identified tensions:

> ... we are developing a code of practice and service level agreements so that we do have an agreed method and practise it. We can refer headteachers to it if there are any disputes but usually we resolve things amicably because we've got to work together at the end of the day ... I do sometimes think I could work in the diplomatic service. I think many [TESS] managers would say the same thing to you.

C explained that occasionally support by a TESS would be negotiated without a formal service level agreement, revealing how complex and resource intensive the process could be:

> What our team does [is that] everybody [in] the peripatetic team has an area of responsibility [in] the county. So they will have an overview of all the schools and the children ... It will be their job to be the liaison with those particular schools, agree with the schools if there's classroom assistant time needed and if we've got it in our budget ... We agree where the [greatest] needs are. Then ... [we] would negotiate with the head, and we don't have a formal bit of paper as a service level agreement, but what we do in actuality ... [is that we] would negotiate with the head and with the class teacher the amount of hours that classroom assistant would have [and] what they would do. So that would be agreed ... [by] us with the school and it would be very clear. They would actually formally write that down and do it.

N synthesised these elements of headteacher-TESS relations, noting that it was generally the headteachers who are less secure who evaded their responsibilities towards Traveller children, whereas confident headteachers were more inclusive:

> ... I think our experience has been that younger heads and new heads feel less secure about taking in children who are clearly different and who don't understand the inclusion aspects. They ... are more likely to come up with the whole range of excuses for not taking children. They give pathetic ones like 'I've got some children in that class with very difficult behaviour'. We say, 'So? You've got a place; the parents want a place'. It's as simple as that, or should be. We've had some of the more experienced – and usually they are older – who are amazingly tolerant – not just tolerant but respectful and inclusive. Tolerant of the situation where of course their school's going to be disrupted if you're going to have six new children for a few days. You tolerate that, but these are people who respect the diversity of the children ... They say, 'Yes, of course they can come. We've got places'. And some will go over numbers to take children in. I think that's more to do with how secure they feel as the leader of the school than age or experience really.

The respondents discussed the Standard Assessment Tasks (SATs) administered to students in England at the ages of 7, 11 and 14, at the end of Key

Stages 1, 2 and 3, to measure students' learning against national standards, as these affected the decisions of headteachers and the work of TESSs.

G asserted that the SATs and published school league tables discouraged the acceptance of Traveller students into schools and collaboration between TESSs and schools:

> [SATs are] a constant source of stress for Traveller teachers because ... the schools ... they've been forced into the situation. We have league tables. Obviously heads are very concerned about SATs. When you've got a child who perhaps has been there for twelve weeks of the year ... he's going to struggle ... It's a real problem because it doesn't reflect the ability of the child. It might reflect his lack of attendance. But it's a cause of problems with schools because schools ... tend to blame the Traveller teachers for what they might perceive as any problems that they have with the Traveller pupils. So it's a fairly regular thing to ... [be blamed] by headteachers or heads of department about children with poor attendance, for whatever reason, whether they've been in the area and just haven't been going to school or whether they've been off and about, both of which are equally possible: 'These people are bringing my results down' ... In fact, headteachers often when SAT time comes around try and dump off the register any Travellers who haven't been for a while in ... [the] hope that it will somehow massage the figures. Obviously not all heads are like that but some are ... I can see their point.

N identified a covert association between government policy and the unwelcoming approaches of some headteachers:

> ... we do see the view, with all the target setting that's going on from central government – if I was a headteacher I would be reluctant to take someone in mid May. The target setting has made it more difficult for heads to be inclusive automatically. To say, ' ... Of course they can come. As long as I don't have to include them in my SATs figures.' The difficulties are compounded ...

K noted the ongoing impact of headteachers' ambivalence towards SATS and Traveller students and the work of TESSs: 'I'm working with the schools with the situation with the target setting and SATs results and things like that now. We have to negotiate a lot with schools where really they should just take them'.

Thus effective and mutually trusting relations between headteachers and TESSs are difficult to establish, located as they are at the intersection between interpersonal emotions and values and formal policies and agreements. Yet TESS heads of service and teachers depend on good relations to carry out their work successfully. R put it starkly:

Some schools are brilliant; some schools are diabolical. There's no two ways about it; it is really hard work in some schools, but some are very, very good. They pick up immediately. It usually stems from the top. If you've got a good headteacher, good senior management team, then the rest of it falls into place, and that's brilliant. If there isn't, there are failing schools.

Implications for practice

Legally, if there is a place available in a non-selective school, then any child should be able to take it up on request. However, headteachers have some discretion and it is they who determine the ethos of their schools and who will feel welcome there. Whatever the hostility towards Travellers where they stop, school should provide a safe haven for their children to learn and grow in a caring atmosphere. Many headteachers ensure that their schools do so for all their students and operate flexibly and inclusively. They are sensitive to the needs of Traveller families, offer support with filling in admission forms, have spare uniforms available to help children fit in, make agreements about the wearing of jewellery, and take dinner money daily if that helps family arrangements. Everything possible is done to make the parents feel that their children will be welcome and safe in the new school.

But others make it difficult for Traveller children to take up school places. They might insist on strict uniform or lengthy admissions procedures involving governors' meetings. Class sizes might be inflexible so that only one place is offered to a family. There are many ways to delay or prevent an admission. TESS staff are all too familiar with being told that a school is suddenly full when they request a place for a Traveller child, and learn how important negotiating skills can be.

Headteachers are caught in their own web of relationships. The local authority, the DfES and Ofsted inspectors demand ever higher standards, parents want attention and resources for their children, the governors have a certain vision for the school and their staff need their support. The standards agenda is hard to reconcile with principles of inclusion, but every school now has written policies on inclusion, equal opportunities, bullying and anti-racism. However, the degree to which those policies are implemented varies. If a school does take in Traveller children, there is too often an anxious telephone call to the TESS: 'I've got Travellers here – give me some help'. This would not be the reaction to the arrival in school of children from any other ethnic minority group. Nevertheless, there may well be a call a few days later expressing relief that the Traveller children are much the same as the other children.

TESS teams take on various roles with schools and headteachers. They encourage and enable schools to discharge their responsibilities to Traveller children and some TESSs make in-service training in the school a condition of their support. Often headteachers expect TESS staff to take responsibilities that they would consider their own if it were other children. The support the TESSs can or feel that they should give may differ from what the school would like. For example, some headteachers expect TESS teachers to assess and then withdraw Traveller children to give them intensive support, separating them from their peer group, whereas most TESSs have policies of in-class provision if direct teaching support is offered at all. Negotiations around this issue can create tensions as we will see. Some headteachers expect the TESS teachers to provide a link between school and home, communicating with parents on behalf of the school. Many TESSs do consider outreach work with families to be an important part of their role but this should not hinder the development of direct relationships between parents and school staff.

There are times when TESS staff have to give immediate attention to a new mobile group that has suddenly arrived in their area and this might necessitate withdrawing support for a while from children already in school. Speed of response is imperative when working with highly mobile groups but schools need to know what support they can rely on. Headteachers may feel let down by services when contact seems unpredictable. To avoid conflicts of interest and misunderstandings, many TESSs negotiate support agreements with schools, which clarify timescales and priorities and the roles and responsibilities of each person involved. The TESS teachers set out the parameters of their support with headteachers and negotiate mutually acceptable ways of working. This is easy to say, but can be fraught with difficulties, and may be exacerbated by relationships of power. Headteachers have increasing autonomy, particularly over budgets, to determine what goes on in their schools, so the support agreements are essential.

The DfES is currently urging TESS teams to change the emphasis of their support from work with individual students to training initiatives with the whole school. The relationships with schools are bound to change as TESS teachers move from being colleagues in the classroom to trainers of ancillary staff, teachers, headteachers and governors. It is important that professional development opportunities are offered to TESS staff, to prepare them for their shifting roles. When they offer in-service training to schools, it may not be taken up. Headteachers have to ensure that their staff stay afloat on a river of initiatives, such as developments in literacy, numeracy, healthy schools and citizenship, which affect all children. They are unlikely to prioritise training around the needs of Traveller children if there are only two or three in the school, despite the anxieties expressed when they first arrive.

Ideally learning about the educational needs of the various Traveller groups should be part of every teacher's professional development, whether or not their school has Traveller children on roll. Because the initial response to parents, the first impressions of the school and the child's experience on the first day are strong determinants of successful inclusion of these children, schools need to understand and respect Traveller cultures before the children set foot in the school. Their experience can then start on a positive note. This is the responsibility of the headteacher, with support from the TESS.

However, statistics and league tables largely determine many headteachers' priorities. When an Ofsted inspection is due, the headteacher may meet one of the TESS team to confirm that the school's provision for the Traveller children is adequate, but the headteacher will also be concerned about attendance figures. Absences for travelling away to fairs may be authorised, but they still show as absences in the data. Allowing dual registration, which enables children to attend other schools when travelling while keeping their main base school place open for their return, has benefited the families but although it demonstrates good practice on the part of the school, it does not look well in the figures.

Headteachers may be concerned about SATs results when admitting children whose schooling has been severely interrupted. A disproportionate number of Traveller children may be disapplied from meeting national curriculum requirements for the sake of the school profile rather than for their own benefit. On the other hand, children arriving in a school for a brief period just before the annual student count day, on which budgets for the year are set, may be welcomed enthusiastically.

All in all, TESS staff have a great deal of work to do in schools and with headteachers before their presence becomes unnecessary.

8

Relations with teachers

The relationships TESS staff form with class teachers are extremely important. They operate on the class teacher's territory so TESS teachers need to be sensitive in another teacher's space, particularly as the role of TESSs begins to change.

Relationships with class teachers are – as with heads – pivotal for TESS heads of service. The diversity of aspiration and experience wherever TESSs work is also apparent in the relationship. The two groups of professionals may know little about each other's students but a smoothly functioning partnership between them is crucial to the learning outcomes of Traveller children. Here too examples abound of innovative and transformative practice in developing these partnerships but there are also undesirable and even obstructive incidents.

The Traveller education literature cites many examples of class teachers failing to facilitate the learning of Traveller students and of the same teachers' less constructive interactions with TESSs. For example, according to Liégeois (1998):

> One of the principal difficulties is teachers' own attitudes. We have already described the negative reception the [Gypsy] Traveller child usually gets in the classroom ... Prejudice leads teachers – including 'specialised' teachers – to believe that there is little or nothing of the children's own culture which could be utilised in the school; their contribution to the class is considered negligible; the majority of teachers show no interest in culturally-based teaching materials despite their recognition of the inappropriateness of the materials they are using. (p219)

Similarly, in her account of Italian *attrazionisti viaggianti*, Gobbo (2006) was critical of schools in which '... educational authorities have done almost nothing ... to make these pupils anything but temporary guests who deserve, but seldom get, enough attention and help from the teachers, as much as the latter would like to give that attention and help' (pp799-800). Gobbo also wrote about '... the indifference of the educational institutions to the diverse abilities, wants and needs that ... [the Travelling children] have or might learn that they have' (p800).

In a summary of a larger study (Derrington and Kendall, 2004), Derrington (2005) listed the factors identified by Traveller children's primary school teachers as likely to make the children's smooth transition into secondary school more difficult:

■ hostile exchanges between teachers and Traveller students

■ Traveller students' direct communication style

■ Traveller students being influenced by others with behavioural difficulties

■ Traveller students masking difficulties and seeking peer approval

■ the absence of a trusted adult

■ Traveller students being pressured to challenge the pecking order of power and influence among the wider student body

■ Traveller students' irregular attendance at school. (pp56-57)

Derrington (2005) found such behaviour among secondary school teachers and heads of year and she observed that some heads of year 'readily attributed the [negative] behaviour to cultural factors rather than the management style of colleagues' (p57). Derrington also noted three factors not identified by their primary school teachers that reduced students' likelihood of completing secondary school:

■ the assignment of detentions for failure to complete homework

■ fractures in the relationship between parents and teachers that had been well-developed in the primary schools

■ evidence of bullying and racism towards the Traveller students (p59)

Derrington's (2005) analysis of this divergence between Traveller students' primary school and secondary school experiences revealed that:

> ... although discourse and expectations around Gypsy Travellers and their engagement with secondary education tend to be dominated by cultural pathology, historical patterns of resistance are constantly challenged or reinforced by positive and

negative experiences. In the vast majority of cases, the students that described themselves as being happy at school successfully completed the first three years. In many cases, parents recognised the benefits of, and maintained positive attitudes about, secondary education and their trust in the school system was put to the test. Once parents believed that their child's social, moral, physical or emotional well-being was under threat and was not being addressed, a breakdown in home-school relationships was likely to ensue and lead, ultimately, to permanent disengagement. (p61)

Bullying and racism, specifically name-calling, were reported by Lloyd and Stead (2001) in their study of Gypsy and Show Traveller students in Scotland. They identified a disparity in teachers' perceptions of these groups but also the varied attitudes of those teachers:

... teachers and managers were much more positive about Show Traveller pupils and much less likely to see them as disruptive. The behaviour of some Gypsy Traveller pupils was often, however, seen as problematic by school staff and several had been excluded from school ... Some teachers contextualised this within an understanding of the culture of Gypsy Travellers; others had little knowledge of Gypsy Travellers' lives or, like the rest of the community, partial, stereotyped or prejudiced views. Equally, lack of knowledge [of], or indeed a rejection, by Gypsy Traveller pupils of school norms and values sometimes underpinned their actions ... (p363)

Lloyd and Stead (2001) cited a telling critique of class teachers' poor reflexivity by a Traveller support teacher:

... I think the shortfall is ... that teachers in schools are not aware of their own culture; they are all dying to be told about Travellers' culture but they are not aware that this is a system that they operate in ... You really have to have a close introspective look at the culture you are creating in a school. (p372)

Finally, one of the action research case stories presented by O'Hanlon and Holmes (2004, pp79-81) reported the results of a survey questionnaire with class teachers in seven primary schools in one LEA. These results reflected a general absence of understanding of Traveller culture and lack of knowledge of LEA and school policies concerning Traveller students. The authors discerned '... a serious omission of Traveller culture in schools' (p84) and contended that class teachers were 'more negative' (p84) than the headteachers of the participating schools: 'either they didn't include Traveller culture or they didn't see the need to include Traveller culture, particularly when Traveller children already attended their schools. Those who did include Traveller culture did so in the same home-in-a-trailer stereotypical manner' (p84).

The literature indicates that class teacher-TESS relations are enacted in a complex context of longstanding and sometimes stereotypical assumptions about Travellers which do not make the work of TESSs easy. As the pressures on class teachers increase, the TESS heads of service and teachers, generally supporting a small number of Traveller students, have greater difficulty establishing productive relationships with class teachers. However, when relationships are positive, effective strategies for teaching Traveller children flourish.

Several participants in the research described examples of practical collaboration between TESS staff members and class teachers. The interpersonal relations between them are analysed in terms of the differing interests and responsibilities of TESSs and schools, which sometimes facilitated effective partnerships but more often created obstacles.

Some respondents echoed the accounts in the literature showing class teachers who have little knowledge of Traveller culture. G, who answered 'Very much so' when asked whether he saw himself as an advocate for Travellers, asserted:

> A lot of what we do is arguing the Travellers' corner in schools, I think ... [Not] necessarily on the big stage ... It's the informal side of things as well. An awful lot of settled people just don't know anything about Travellers, and teachers are no different. They're very ignorant, in the nicest possible way; they just don't know anything. Why should they?

Effective relations depend on mutual empathy and respect. B said sympathetically:

> Being ... Traveller teacher[s], we don't have as much paperwork and as many things to sort out as a class teacher has to do. The [latter's] workload is just phenomenal. I ... [left classroom teaching] just before the national curriculum came in.

Respondents mentioned a particular obstacle to establishing strong relations with class teachers. There was no continuity and they had to develop rapport with new teachers each year. O said:

> ... I tend to deal with a teacher at that time, and then next year deal with another teacher, because it doesn't get passed on. People are so busy [that] they don't want to know if it's something they don't need to know about now. So when I come the following year, they will deal with that [then].

N perceived that some class teachers lacked confidence:

> ... some teachers never feel confident of themselves as teachers to have support teachers in the room and working in a more flexible way. That's a shame but it's a

reality and we can work away at it, but we can't expect to be invited in immediately. I think that the relationship we as support teachers have with class teachers is different every time ...

F articulated both the tensions and the benefits in building partnerships between TESSs and class teachers:

> ... [TESS teachers have] got to know exactly what they're talking about before they go into schools, because if they don't know as much [as] or more than the class teacher they're in trouble. I try to make sure that the staff here know more about what's been expected from the national curriculum than the class teacher does ... We may not have the in-depth knowledge; we need that from the class teacher. That's why we like to try our materials for distance learning back with the class teachers in schools, because they're the ones who can feed that in. So it's got to be a two-way process. We have no problems in terms of that.

When we analysed the practical strategies for establishing effective relations between TESSs and class teachers, we found examples of TESSs's initiative and innovation but also how systemic pressures affect their interactions with schools. Some strategies were opportunistic: 'When you go into schools, you have a good relationship with the school staff ... A lot gets done in the staffroom at coffee time' (Interview C). Others were more systematic and long-term, for instance, keeping a record for Traveller children who are in schools for very short periods, for which the TESSs and schools take different but complementary responsibilities:

> We have this sheet which is a short stay report form, so if children are only in a school for a couple of days, or three weeks, and they're mobile children, we would go into the school with this, and we'd ask the class teacher to complete this ... Then when they go, the school keeps a copy of these [forms] [and] we have a copy, so that if the next school phones up ... – the [previous] class teacher has this [and] it's very easy to fax that through ... [This] gives ... immediate ... [information]. (Interview C)

While most TESSs emphasised that their role was to provide support rather than to teach individual Traveller children in schools, this varied from one TESS to another and was not always easy to communicate to class teachers. N reported:

> Because some of the children have had gaps in their learning we will be giving direct pupil support, so we've been working to identify the gaps ..., and have a kind of accelerated learning program alongside them, being in the class most of the time, alongside the class teacher, working with the class. That's our preferred way of giving direct pupil support, but every situation really is leading towards very low levels of support, where we're supporting the school rather than the child. So that we're showing them some of the things we've learned along the way about how you

include children who might be at a different level of achievement, who have a different experience that they bring to school.

F outlined an innovative variation on in-service training that facilitated sustained contact and collaboration between the TESS teachers and class teachers:

> ... I've got a bit of extra money from the DfEE for in-service, and I try to use it so that the in-service training I do ... with teachers; it's not the way you normally do in-service training ... When we negotiate the project, I will go down to the school with our coordinator and the teacher who is going to do it, and we will meet senior management in the school and the teacher who's going to teach it. We will work out what the aims are of what it is we're trying to do. We'll make sure that this is a partnership, that there is work going to be done on both sides, that it will be written up properly afterwards and that we will have planning built into it. So I pay for the cover [teacher release time] for that. Then I pay for the cover for my teacher and the teacher from the school to spend half a day or a day planning it. And the same at the end. And if necessary, a bit in between ... [T]he class teacher will fax our teacher here with what she's going to be teaching. Our teacher here will then do her bit in terms of materials, so that when they're working in the classroom they both know exactly what it is that they're doing ... That way you're actually recognising the professionalism of the class teacher, and giving them something that they don't normally get. The same with the teacher here. Because I really do think teachers coming out here for a day ... What works much better is being able to work alongside a teacher in a classroom, and to be able to allow that teacher some thinking time and to be able to put into operation some of the things they would like to do if they had another pair of hands in the classroom.

Speaking about the need to distinguish among different forms of support to be provided by TESS staff members, E said:

> One of the things I think we've developed successfully here is an ability to look at a learning situation and to assess who it is that needs the support in that situation: is it the child ... who requires support in terms of induction into the school, into the social context, the routine? Is it the child who needs learning support, or is it in fact the curriculum that needs development and adaptation to allow access by the teacher? Is it the class teacher who needs support to understand this child as an early learner? ... Some class teachers ... are incredibly worried if they don't make up the gaps in the child's learning within the four week stretch ... that they're in the school. Then those class teachers who say they're only here for four weeks, [so] why bother? We need to have the ability to say, 'Where do we need to put in the support, and what kind of support do we need to put in?'.

TESS heads of service and teachers have to draw on their varied skills to facilitate effective relations with class teachers, just as they do with headteachers.

Relations can be tentative and temporary or, at worst, uncomprehending and obstructive. But they can also be enduring and harmonious, underpinning the development of innovative approaches to providing TESS support for Traveller children and class teachers and creating new professional energy. As J asserted: '... the [TESS] primary teacher has given the class teachers confidence and support with those [Traveller] pupils and themselves with materials and suggestions, being ... experienced teacher[s] themselves. So it's been that sharing of professionalism and modelling good practice ...'. E noted: 'It's about giving people the confidence to try new things ... There's got to be that permission to make mistakes if we're actually going to make progress ... [It's] about ways in which we can develop collaborative working and shared responsibilities for development ...'.

Implications for practice

Traveller children come into schools in many different circumstances and for varying lengths of time. Some of them, whose parents are more or less settled on a site or in housing and seldom travel, will attend school on a fairly permanent basis. Others have one school as their regular base school, say for the winter months, and then travel away seasonally with their families. When the seasonal travelling routes are the same each year, the children may come into schools regularly for brief periods. The travelling patterns of other families are not fixed and the time they stay in each place depends on a number of factors. Children in these families can only go into schools for short- or medium-term stays. Some circus children or Travellers subjected to swift evictions may access a school for only two or three days, while others may stay for several weeks. For families who have no site place at all and who spend the whole year moving from one location to another, staying as long as the work lasts or the unofficial stopping place is tolerated, access to school and length of stay are unpredictable. Travellers living in housing may not be settled and will often move between houses or go from house to trailer and back again, with consequent changes of school.

The children in these different situations have a wide range of needs and it is up to the class teacher, with support from TESS teachers, to give each child as constructive a school experience as possible in the time available. Some teachers feel that it is hardly worth it to take children in to their class for only a couple of days, but the effect of school experience is cumulative. Every positive experience, every welcome will help to engage children with education and make them eager to attend the next school, where they might have more time. A succession of bad days may result in their dropping out altogether.

However, it is difficult to decide what is best for each child in a limited period, and having the resources to deliver it is a further challenge. And every class teacher has their own way of working, using support and organising the classroom, which has to be accommodated by the TESS teacher. Sharing another teacher's space is never easy and must be done sensitively.

TESS support teachers can fulfil many roles in a classroom and there is the potential for confusion or tension between them and the class teacher if agreements have not been made in advance. Many TESS negotiate support agreements with headteachers before entering the classroom but the busy class teachers still often assume that they will withdraw the Traveller children to give them focused attention, although this is seldom done. Preparation and information are as important for the class teacher as they are for the child. Preliminary visits to school are invaluable for child, parent and class teacher alike, but are not always possible. Some families carry their children's education record books with them, detailing previous assessments or work done and targets set in other schools, hoping to avoid a continual round of assessments or repetition of work. TESSs have established record exchange schemes to give class teachers rapid access to relevant information about their new students. These can be an excellent starting point for teachers, but only if they are easy to understand and up to date, and if the receiving teacher has time to build constructively on the information.

Class teachers may have some notice that Traveller children are arriving; they may have seen the same children, or others like them, before. They may have some records to look at; they may have a chance for some planning and preparation in advance in cooperation with a TESS teacher. On the other hand, they may never have had a Traveller child in their class before a family turns up at school and asks for the children to be admitted. Whatever the circumstances, they need to be prepared to include the Traveller children in the same way that they would welcome any new child to the class. The challenge for TESS teachers is how they can best support school staff in achieving this inclusion.

There are various ways in which a support teacher might work with children in school (see Chapter 3) – withdrawal of individuals or groups, in-class support, support in a mixed group, help with assessments and target setting, differentiation of materials, giving the class teacher time to work with the Traveller children and so on. Some TESSs have prepared induction packs for children who are new to school which may be helpful to the class teacher. All these methods have been or are still in use in schools. But there are increasing demands on TESS teachers' time; they cannot be in all schools supporting individuals or small groups. And ultimately that does not contribute to the professional development of the class teachers enabling them to include the Traveller children without support.

Some TESSs focus on in-service training, increasingly encouraged by the DfES. The training offers greater understanding of the particular needs of different travelling groups. For instance, children from the circus may come into one school for only three or four days on their tour. But this is the children's experience every week and they are well used to adapting to new school routines. For them a new school is the norm; their presence is only a novelty to the receiving school. Their needs are to get into class and get down to the work that the other children are doing with little fuss. Fairground children may be carrying distance learning packs of work with them, prepared by their winter base school teachers and TESS staff. They need the work to be checked and to have help with identified problem areas, while being integrated as much as possible into the work of the class.

It is important for class teachers to understand that a child who shows minimal literacy skills could well be bright but has had few opportunities to learn to read. They do not need slow paced remedial support, but a concentrated catch-up programme. The identification of special needs, or the fact that the child does not have a learning difficulty, is problematic in a short time scale. However, a knowledge of the children's circumstances and travelling patterns may give clues to their opportunities for formal education, so direct relationships with parents are important.

TESSs also support schools and class teachers through curriculum development. Many TESSs have created fiction and non-fiction books, photo packs, puzzles, posters, worksheets and all kinds of materials based in the various Traveller cultures. But many class teachers find out about them only when Traveller children come into school and someone from the TESS brings them in as support materials. Class teachers generally use the materials only with the Traveller children, and this is unhelpful. Though it is good for the children to see their culture represented and respected in school, it is counterproductive if it makes the children seem strange or exotic to the rest of the class. Such materials need to be in the classroom already and to be familiar to all the children, so that the arrival of a Traveller child is nothing untoward.

How can this be done? Class teachers are busy with training on a range of issues and may resent spending time on an issue that seems irrelevant. Many of the materials developed by TESSs have small print runs and lack the advantage of a distribution network. To overcome these difficulties some TESSs have sought relationships with mainstream publishers, urging them to produce story books which will relate to the lives of Travellers. Others have worked in partnership with literacy consultants and other subject education advisers to include Traveller cultures, histories, images and issues within the curriculum materials for all. These initiatives all have great scope for development.

The recent government proposal for personalised learning set out in a White Paper (DfES, 2005) has a vision to provide for all children's needs and promises budget support to realise it. Personalised learning is about providing a tailored education for every child. It starts from an in-depth understanding of their individual needs, provides relevant and challenging opportunities that match their needs, and supports them to flourish and progress in their learning and development. This must include Traveller children.

Part 5:
Innovations in curriculum practice

9

Innovations in teaching literacy

Much literature on literacy deals with stages of progression and how to overcome difficulties. But the reason why Traveller children may be unable to read at 14 may have nothing to do with ability. It may simply be lack of access to learning. So the matter has to be addressed in particular ways and TESSs have developed many innovative projects.

We turn finally to innovative curriculum practice. This and the following chapter clearly show Traveller educators as educational pioneers whose innovative solutions to the distinctive needs and problems of mobile students have transformed students' life chances and lives.

Denning (2004) points out that 'an innovation is a transformation of practice in a community' and is not necessarily the same as 'the invention of a new idea or object' (p1). He also argued that 'a transformation of practice in a community won't happen unless the new practice generates more value to the members than the old' (p2) and that both personal practices and organisational processes are crucial for establishing a culture of innovation. The innovations presented in this and the following chapter fulfil Denning's parameters because:

■ they were forged in the fires of the TESS staff members' enacted professional practice

■ they were located at the intersection of the personal practices of TESS staff members and the organisational processes of TESSs

■ they are not easily transferable to other educational sites or situations.

The innovations under scrutiny are teaching literacy in this chapter and in the next chapter using educational technologies. We could have included other innovations by Traveller educators, such as their approaches to educational leadership and professional learning, but we focus on literacy and technologies because they are vital to facilitating the learning of Traveller children and they reflect TESS staff members' effectiveness in helping transform their learning opportunities.

The literacy literature is vast and growing. Although we do not downplay the importance of 'cognitive, technical or behavioural characteristics and skills' (Henderson, 2005), we highlight the sociocultural dimension of literacy:

> Being literate is much more than knowing how to read and write in a standardised, unitary way. It is about being able to engage in particular literate practices, using the conventions that are regarded as appropriate for particular contexts ... Success or failure in literacy learning, then, is not independent of social, cultural, moral and political relationships and can be conceptualised in terms of access to and engagement in particular literate practices... (p10)

One crucial consequence for Traveller children of these 'social, cultural, moral and political relationships' is that 'being literate' takes place in two separate and for them potentially contradictory locations: at home and at school. Therefore Traveller educators have to find innovative ways to help them negotiate effective and meaningful pathways between these two locations and establish sustainable links between home and school literacy that they can take into their adult lives. As Henderson (2005) avers:

> Literacy teaching, too, is a social practice and a political, not neutral, activity. Teachers play an instrumental role in the selection, construction and distribution of particular types of literacy, in socialising students into particular versions of the world, and in deciding what constitutes satisfactory literacy performance. (p11)

The Traveller education literature contains several accounts of literacy learning and teaching, including some references to innovative ways of bridging the worlds of home and school. Liégeois (1998) argued that 'the Gypsy experience provides a paradigm with much to offer other minorities and indeed all school-related issues' (p14), claiming that 'the Gypsy paradigm appears to be an exceptionally innovative one' (p15). But Liégeois recognises that innovative capacity as it applies to mobile learners' linguistic ability may not be valued by school systems:

> But if Gypsy linguistic practice cannot be ignored in school, pedagogy based on its dynamics, or even a simple recognition of its legitimacy, is still far from widespread. On the contrary, the children's use of language is still on the whole viewed as an

obstacle to be overcome before even basic learning (reading and writing) can be accomplished – in the official national language. (p199)

O'Hanlon and Holmes (2004, pp125-131) feature a case study related to literacy. A Traveller educator investigated three primary schools and tried to negotiate appropriate provision for Traveller students in the context of competing expectations of class teachers and her line manager, and in a broader framework of the National Literacy Strategy and the literacy hour. Their conclusion is telling:

> The investigation was successful in raising the profile of Traveller children within the LEA, but it needed more status and support from LEA management to initiate the changes necessary to significantly raise standards. Schools must recognise Travellers as a distinct culture and make moves to respond to them, not try to force Traveller children to fit the existing systems ... It is necessary to have a whole school approach to raising standards and to ensure that this addresses Traveller children's needs and thus improves literacy skills within the Traveller community. (p131)

Wood (2005) outlined the genesis and evaluation of Literacy for All, a particularly successful set of initiatives associated with Traveller education and the National Literacy Strategy implemented by the Cambridgeshire Race Equality and Diversity Service in partnership with local schools at Key Stage 2. Wood was clear about the reasons for the success of this curriculum innovation:

> High quality texts, focused planning, activities that drew on children's own experiences, opportunities for speaking and listening, and writing for a purpose were among the factors that have motivated pupils and teachers alike. Everyone agrees that partnership working at every level is making a real difference where it counts, in schools with individual classteachers and crucially with children of all minority and majority backgrounds. (p90)

One noteworthy 'high quality text' was *Gypsies and Travellers in Their Own Words: Words and Pictures of Travelling Life* (Saunders *et al*, 2000). It contained 'sixteen main stories and the themes of camps and sites, family photographic collections and the history of local Fairs which interweave the stories' (pxiii). Such creativity in enhancing Traveller children's literacy learning and its broader applicability for teaching other students are welcome but not surprising. It fits Denning's (2004) notion of innovation as transformation of practice, with the examples of curriculum innovation outlined below and also with Henderson's (2005) telling challenge to contemporary educators:

> In moving beyond the view that under-achievement is inevitable or predictable for itinerant students, teachers should be better placed to focus on responsive and flexible pedagogies for enabling children to achieve demonstrable and sustainable learning outcomes in school literacy learning. (p385)

The interviews in the study matched the situated and politicised character of literacy outlined above. They also provided examples of innovative approaches to literacy teaching by TESSs. These innovative approaches emerged despite the wide diversity of views among TESS staff members. Some took the view that despite the rich cultural heritage of Travellers – which they praised – the children's prior and informal literacy at home made it difficult for the children to engage with the formal literacy of school: '... that is a drawback if you're looking for high success at school because you need the home and the school to work very closely together to really encourage that child' (Interview U).

Others focused on the intention and implementation of the literacy hour and again views diverged. Some interviewees regarded it as an opportunity to highlight Traveller education issues with schools, whereas others perceived it as too inflexible and generic to facilitate their efforts to work collaboratively with schools. Some were ambivalent: 'I'm still waiting to see, really. I think it's more inclusive. How we support it we're still coming to terms with' (Interview S).

There were many kinds of curriculum innovation but we can only deal with three here. They are of three types:

- specialised materials for the literacy hour
- dedicated support for Traveller secondary students
- consolidated relations between TESSs and schools

The common denominator is the determination of TESS heads of service and teachers to seize any opportunity to advance the interests of Traveller children in an educational system that contains spaces for doing so but is too large and centralised to make it easy. As D remarked:

> ... you have to try and get to grips with all the different initiatives that there are and ... make the connections ... So it's a question of trying to keep up with knowing what's going on, reading all the documents and just all the time trying to understand ... what your central aim is ... [and how you] can make the relevant connections. That's essentially what we try to do.

Several TESSs embraced the literacy hour to develop specialised materials that present a positive, non-stereotypical view of the heritage and culture of Travellers. This fits Denning's (2004) conceptualisation of innovation as transformation of practice, emerging from the complex intersection of contexts attending the literacy hour and the possibilities and constraints of school-based approaches to literacy teaching, including that of for Traveller children.

The literacy hour created an unprecedented opportunity for TESSs to promote the use of resource materials that contested stereotyped images of Travellers. As one participant said:

> A lot of primary schools are into these big reading books. There's more of those that are Traveller friendly now, so we are actually showing schools that there are materials that we can actually loan them ... These will incorporate Travellers more into the literacy hour. From that point of view, we're trying to do our bit on the cultural front. (Interview I)

J was equally positive:

> ... in a school where they have quite a strong Gypsy Traveller population, there was a genuine concern from staff ... that the children's levels of ability were much lower than the rest, and how were they going to teach them within the classroom? The suggestion at the beginning of the year was that we should have a separate Traveller literacy hour ... [W]e were saying we felt that the [Traveller] children should still be within their class groups. It took some negotiation and some working together, and one authority ... produced a really helpful booklet, *The Literacy Hour and Traveller Children*. That gave evidence and backup that yes, it could work. I'm pleased to say that in that particular school now I feel as though we're working really well together.

Two respondents spoke about innovative approaches to supporting Traveller children's literacy learning at the secondary school level (see also Derrington and Kendall, 2004). One related to the development of literacy support materials for Traveller students in secondary schools:

> I've tried to look at the different phases because sometimes the secondary is a concern, and yes, we have got funding for secondary as well. It's having age appropriate materials to work with the secondary Travellers. They might still have quite basic needs when it does come to literacy ... We try to build in a cultural aspect of it as well with materials to be developed both nationally and ... from regional meetings I go to ... I've just ordered three photo packs from one authority. One, for example, is based around a scrap yard because a lot of our families work in that area. Wonderful photographs; lovely stimulus for language. One about homes and one about animals. (Interview J)

The other approach focused on Traveller students in year seven, the first year of secondary school:

> Now at secondary [level] we've tried to do quite a lot of work with year seven. We do slightly different work at secondary. Apart from the settling in and the distance learning, we do try a lot of differentiation work. We've tried to hone that into year seven, because obviously what we need is to keep children in until year seven. If they can't understand the materials that they've been given then they're not going

to stay because they become bored. So we have tried to work on the literacy level. (Interview F)

A third innovative approach to Traveller children's literacy learning and teaching centred on consolidating productive partnerships between TESSs and schools. According to T:

... I think [that] with the literacy hour it does make it quite clear that it is to include all children ... so I see it as a great step forward ... So I feel when I do work in [the] literacy hour I work quite closely with the teachers, and we know what we want to get out [of it]. I think it works well.

B used professional development opportunities arising from the literacy hour to strengthen collegial relations with local schools and teachers:

... often, when the advice the county sends out ... [about] various courses, they don't realise we exist. So it's very handy. I have a base school, and so I say, 'What's new? What's going on? Can I be included in it, please?'. And that's the way often [that] we have the literacy hour training through the base school.

L's TESS had initiated new role descriptions for TESS staff members related to the literacy hour that would emphasise how they could enhance Traveller students' literacy and learning outcomes:

... we're just completing a document that we were hoping to use within schools ... suggesting ways support staff might be used in the literacy hour ... In there we're suggesting literally on a tick chart the sorts of roles that support teachers and our learning support assistants ... might take in the different elements of the literacy hour. So obviously we're being proactive there in saying to the school staff, 'Look, we appreciate there's pressures on you, that this literacy hour has got various elements to it. We can fit in and we can work in different ways and in different elements'.

Curriculum innovation in response to Traveller education and the literacy hour involved negotiation on multiple fronts. P related how:

We came to various compromises. All the compromises were different in different schools ... Basically we've just negotiated with the schools, and we are now doing what we call 'catch up'. Say, for example, we've got an 8 year-old child who really is only at 6 or 7 year-old level. What we're doing is, we're putting support into the literacy hour by withdrawal [of Traveller students] during the plenary, the last bit [of the literacy hour]. We're also sending in resources and some teaching time for an afternoon session so that they can catch up what they've missed, and it's basically like a colander, trying to plug all the little holes up before they move onto the next level. That is how we've had so much success with our SATs results. But it took a lot of negotiation, really.

TESS staff members' approaches to Traveller children's literacy learning and teaching, particularly in the context of the advent of the literacy hour, are often models of Denning's (2004) conceptualisation of innovation as transformation of practice. But they are seldom easy and not necessarily permanent. What they do show is Traveller educators operating as educational pioneers, working against the odds to seize opportunities and create strategies that help to construct alternative and enabling futures for Travellers and other children. As L emphasised:

> We've always constantly made reference to what teachers want of us, and we consciously respond to those needs. I think that's the strength of the project. We're heavily invested into the education of particularly Traveller children, but obviously the education of all children, the framework within which we operate. Hence our responses to the literacy hour; hence our responses to target setting and continuity. That's really the message I'd hope you'd be able to take away.

Implications for practice

The issue of literacy and Traveller children is complex. For many parents literacy is the prime reason for sending children to school and they expect that this will be achieved without undue delay. Indeed, some children do progress quickly when they can attend school regularly. Able children who have been denied access to education seize the opportunity to learn. However, it is rarely so straightforward. Much depends on whether the children have had any preschool experience, the age at which they have the chance to start school, their degree of mobility, their attitude and their experience in school.

Traveller children rarely have space to keep books at home, nor do the predominantly oral cultures have much use for books. Many Traveller parents have developed strategies for coping despite their own low literacy, but they see the need for literacy in contemporary society and want their children to have the chance to learn to read and write, in addition to the education they get at home. Teachers of young Traveller children may have to start by familiarising children with books and the printed word and developing their understanding of how stories are shared through text and pictures.

The issue of language and vocabulary then arises, as the settings of many stories will not be familiar to the children. All children need to understand the context and vocabulary of a story. Reading schemes and stories that bear no relationship to their lives are unlikely to engage them. Accordingly, many TESS teachers developed their own materials, incorporating words and situations they knew to be relevant to the children. One TESS wrote a complete initial literacy scheme for use with Traveller children.

The use of Romani words in reading materials designed for Gypsy Traveller children has caused much debate. Some teachers see it as a natural extension of culturally relevant reading materials, and some parents and children have been delighted to find words from their own language in books in school. Indeed, Gypsy Travellers have published their own stories for use in school. Other Traveller parents, however, have expressed annoyance at the use by outsiders of what they consider a private language. As always, teachers need to communicate with parents and to take account of the feelings of the families with whom they work.

The older the children are when they have their first opportunities to learn to read, the harder it will be. They are vulnerable to taunts from their peers about being unable to read, and hide their feelings of inadequacy and embarrassment beneath a veneer of indifference and being unwilling to engage. They certainly do not want to be seen reading 'baby' books. Some teachers have used a language experience approach, encouraging children to tell their own stories, and turning them into texts, which are used as reading material for language games and analysis. The vocabulary and emotional content are thus appropriate for the child. Many teachers have used computers and digital cameras to produce attractive and engaging materials.

However, using specially designed materials implies separate teaching for the Traveller child and heightens the sense of the child being different from the rest of the class. Neither do they take the phonic approach promoted through the literacy hour. The literacy hour has created new challenges and possibilities for the integration of Traveller children. On the one hand, the fact that they will encounter the same structured approach in every school could be reassuring to a mobile student. The familiar routine is a strong argument for the Traveller child being included in the literacy hour. But the inexorable progression of the approach will leave children whose schooling is constantly interrupted with many gaps to fill.

TESS and class teachers have responded in various ways. Some TESSs have created Traveller-friendly stories, posters and other reading materials that are suitable for the whole class to use in the literacy hour. But it is one thing to have developed the resources and another to persuade class teachers to use them. The other drawback is that distribution is seldom wide enough for the materials to be available in a range of schools. Some TESSs have worked with mainstream publishers to enable such distribution. Others have collaborated with library services and literacy consultants, creating lists of existing materials which not only include Traveller children but also raise awareness among other children in the class of the distinct Traveller cultures. TESS staff have contributed alongside literacy consultants to in-service training sessions for teachers and have produced booklets of guidance to good practice. Some have focused on the group activity part of the literacy hour, differentiating materials for particular groups of children. The fact that the whole class is divided into groups working on materials at different levels is an integrating factor and does not expose the Traveller children. For TESS support teachers to make best use of their time within the structure of the hour, careful preparation and planning with the class teacher are vital.

For those whose time in school is often interrupted, the maintenance of records and setting of SMART (Specific, Measurable, Achievable, Relevant, Time-related) targets is also crucial. If class teachers have a basic assessment and record of achievement for the child, they can build on it step by step using small and realistic targets for the length of time that the child is in their class. They are also consolidating the ground on which the next teacher can continue to build. A little focused attention on the child will also help teachers to make the difficult judgment of distinguishing between a lack of learning opportunity and a real learning difficulty.

There are many national and local initiatives to promote literacy, such as homework support clubs, projects linked to sports training and literacy summer schools for those leaving year six. As ever for Traveller children, it is a question of information and realistic access to the opportunities, together with parental permission and support. Despite all efforts, there are still Travellers who reach 14 or 15 without fluent literacy. Helping these young people is yet another challenge for schools and TESSs.

Teenage Travellers who cannot read may have lost the desire to learn in a school context. They will have developed compensatory mechanisms for surviving in their daily lives and may be apprenticed to their families' working practices. Image and status within the peer group are likely to be more important now than struggling to learn to read and write. Methods employed in adult basic education classes would probably be most appropriate for these young people, but schools can seldom provide the safe environment of a group of motivated adults all at similar levels and seeking to improve their skills. A group of TESSs produced a teenage reading pack collaboratively for those who are still motivated to learn, based around a specially written paperback novel (NATT, 1996). This was enabled by DfES development project funding and provided contemporary, relevant materials to use with this particular group.

Some Travellers have been motivated to return to learning as adults and TESSs have instigated several adult literacy projects. Other services have supported access for Travellers to community adult basic education classes in their areas. The involvement of families in projects involving information and communication technology (ICT) (discussed in the next chapter) has also been successful in bringing a number of parents back to learning as they have supported their children in coming to grips with new technologies. The innovative approaches demonstrated by TESS teams to promote literacy for Travellers of all ages are a testament to their imagination and commitment.

10

Innovations in using educational technologies

Among other technological innovations, TESSs have pioneered distance learning for school-age students, especially for fairground and circus children using ICT in England. The particular circumstances of mobility, interrupted schooling and lack of access to a regular electricity supply have provoked a number of imaginative and successful strategies.

Just as literacy traverses the two worlds of home and school in Traveller education, so too do technologies cross multiple locations. Innovation or 'transformation of practice in a community' (Denning, 2004, p1) entails finding new and effective ways of bringing together learners and teachers who are physically separated in space and time through technology. Technology is key to maximising the learning outcomes of the Traveller children so they can fulfil their educational potential.

The literature on educational technologies tends to focus on ICT and particularly on computers in education. But how technologies – in the broadest sense – highlight the innovative actions of TESS heads of service and teachers and their counterparts in schools is often disregarded. The distance learning packs (discussed in Chapters 2, 4 and 8), for example, evolved over place and time in response to the itineraries of different groups of Travellers. Technologies featured here include the networks of human and non-human associations connected with the pedagogical practices situated in the lifeworlds of the Traveller students and their teachers.

We found that the technologies cannot be efficient unless the Traveller families, the TESSs and the base schools are in a harmonious partnership. As O'Hanlon and Holmes (2004) noted, 'school based distance learning can vary in content, quality and presentation' (p43) but 'innovations continue to be developed' (p43). These innovations, they note, are more likely to be sustainable if pre-requisites to school based distance learning are an effective continuity strategy. They identify the pre-requisites, for example that 'work is differentiated according to individual students' needs' and that 'pupils have a consistent network of visiting teachers as they travel, to monitor and support them with their work' (p47). At the heart are responsive and open relationships that use technologies like e-mail to keep up to date with information. But as O'Hanlon and Holmes noted, groups such as some circus families and Gypsy Travellers and people with no legal place to stay, have no access to a base school, and this makes implementing distance learning difficult.

The innovative approaches to educational technologies by TESS staff members have focused on the interpersonal as well as the technical dimensions of technology. What began for the Devon Consortium Traveller Education Service as the search 'for a workable solution to what were perceived as primarily logistical problems dealing with the facts and exigencies of mobility' (Kiddle, 2000) was transformed into the recognition 'that attitudinal issues were equally if not more important' (p270). The Traveller parents needed convincing that distance learning was viable in the context of their lifestyle. Accordingly:

> ... on their own the materials and the technology are not enough. The support systems that engage tutors, teachers, parents and children in active partnerships through an interlocking set of relationships (parent/child, parent/base school teacher, parent/peripatetic teacher, base school teacher/child, peripatetic teacher/ child, base school teacher/peripatetic teacher, etc.) are vital for the learning to take place and for the child's right to an effective full-time education to be honoured. (Kiddle, 1999, p112)

The significance of this complex web of interconnections was evident also in discussions of the important work done by EFECOT and its partner organisations in developing innovative applications of educational technologies for Traveller students. Projects ran throughout the 1990s, principally TOPILOT, FLEX and Trapeze (Marks, 2005, p130; see also Marks, 2003). They combined technologies such as CDI players and satellite to broaden access to formal schooling for mobile groups in several European countries. According to Marks (2005), although, '... as is often the case with leading edge work, the main projects ... did not bear immediate fruit' (p130), '... the projects ... raised awareness about what could be achieved, and they involved a small numbers of TESs ..., with staff gaining direct experience of communication technologies and developing related ICT skills' (p131).

The EFECOT projects provided a sustainable launchpad for the British innovations known as the 'E-learning and Mobility Projects' (E-LAMP) (Tyler, 2005, p132; see also Marks 2004). Currently in its fourth phase, E-LAMP has involved a number of TESSs and base schools which issue laptops and data cards to Traveller children, who can then receive and send information from and to their teachers via the Internet. The mother of one student described how he used his laptop:

> Michael is supplied with a laptop and textbooks. He works on his subjects and then e-mails coursework to his teacher ... [at his base school] for marking. The laptop has a mobile card so, as long as there is coverage, he can submit work. Traveller Education pays for the connection, allowing unlimited time so he can use good websites like Education City. (cited in Hatch, 2006, p24)

The Traveller education literature demonstrates how TESS staff have led innovation in educational technologies as in literacy. And here too are strong resonances between TESS work with technologies and Denning's (2004) 'innovation as transformation of practice'. But we should not forget that fixed residence is still the default mode in contemporary schooling and that technological benefits for mobile groups are not necessarily permanent or evenly distributed:

> ... research reveals the inequalities in access to new technologies within different socioeconomic and class groups ... What is sure is that how Travellers will fare will depend as much on the development of empowering and supportive partnerships between the providers and the Traveller client groups as on any specific resources or policies. (Jordan, 2000, p.261)

The complex mix of innovation – transformed practice – that emanates from productive partnerships using educational technologies for Traveller education and the effect of obstacles to it were strongly evident in the interviews. One TESS, for example, described how it deployed technology for team members to communicate with one another and keep track of the diverse itineraries of the Traveller children in their charge. 'Four of us, we're managing gradually to built up the IT so ... [certain team members] have got laptops and the e-mail facility. So ... [one colleague] and I keep in touch with each other all the time by e-mail' (Interview C). This respondent went on:

> ... essentially what's on the children's sheets we've got on the database. The software's been made for us by the county. So we update that ... as soon as we can

from any changes in here [on the paper-based sheets]. So that will indicate child, date of birth, where they are, what school they're at or if they're on distance learning or if they're doing Education Otherwise, it will indicate what education provision and whether they get any support. That will show on the screen. There's a screen that will come up for the child, and it will show the last five pages. When they go out from us it will indicate 'out of county', so you'll be able to see 'this school', 'out of county' or whatever and then the current [status] will be there. (Interview C)

This might appear fairly mundane but closer examination reveals two examples of using contemporary technologies in ways that make sense in the context of that TESS's work patterns and relationships. This requires effective partnerships among TESS staff members whose mobility parallels that of their students; the technologies must be suited to their lifeworlds.

Respondents' accounts of the distance learning packs created for Traveller children also stressed the importance of relationships. But difficulties arose when the learning packs' pedagogical purpose failed to take account of the children's mobility:

The problem we have at the moment with distance learning is there isn't any inter-action. We send out a learning pack with the kids, and you might hear back from them if they're really keen, but you might not. Then you've lost that opportunity. Some families are very good about returning work, and some families aren't ... (Interview S)

An initiative using relatively simple technologies enhanced Traveller children's motivation to complete the distance learning packs because it established a productive partnership around the children's learning circumstances:

So as a region we tried to put together a sort of reward system. So we have this system of cards with stickers, and if you fill your card up with stickers then you get a CD token. That's sponsored by ... our regional Showmen's Guild. I don't know how much it's costing them – not all that much, I wouldn't think. That's worked fairly well. We wanted a chance to build on that and expand it nationally because we do keep getting inquiries. 'We've got this kid with this card ... He wants a sticker.' I said, 'Well, give him a sticker, any sticker. It doesn't have to be one of our stickers'. 'Oh, no, he wants ... [your] sticker.' (Interview S)

The interplay between technological problems and innovations was affected by the Travellers' mobile lives. One interviewee reported:

I managed to get a computer out of the authority to work with, but we could only run the computer when the elephants' water was being heated, and they didn't always tell us when they were going to turn it on. We had to get a generator running to heat the elephants' water because they had warm water, so while they were doing that we could have the computer working. (Interview S)

Again, relationships were crucial:

What we're looking at now is the use of ICT. We're thinking that one family ... are going to be able to take a laptop with them which we've bought out of our under-spend money. It's a family that we know quite well and trust. We know that there won't be any problems ... We know this family are in a position to take good care of it, so we're doing that. (Interview I)

Partnerships between the TESS and teachers in the base schools were equally important:

... the schools come to us and say, 'Can you help us with the distance learning children when they leave?'. We've tried to shift that onus over the years away from us doing it for them to us advising them to do it for their children. So what we are saying to them is, 'Our experience and our methods show that this way of re-interpreting the curriculum that you'll be covering over the next months – this is the best way of doing that'. Letting them do the job of work, but we would provide expertise, sometimes even material resources. (Interview L)

Other respondents saw how the national curriculum would benefit networking at national and regional levels by TESS and school staff:

... I used to be of the view that the distance learning does have to be very focused on the child, and for that particular child. However, with the national curriculum, it does seem to me that there should be more opportunity for off the shelf distance learning, because everybody's inventing the wheel – everybody's producing the same sort of thing. Although I try to make it very good quality ... It would be really good to have at least core subjects with really good distance learning material for maybe three levels within a year group or a subject or whatever, that one could just take off the shelf and say, 'That's fine; you can have that this time'. Or adjust something. (Interview O)

The interviewees discussed the role of EFECOT in coordinating and sponsoring international projects designed to use educational technologies innovatively to enhance Travellers' learning outcomes. They spoke about the problems caused by technical difficulties and by having to choose among competing needs when resources were so scarce. It took time before families gained access to the applications needed to use those technologies. S commented that:

... with the CDI ... there isn't that sort of involvement with technology on the fairgrounds that would allow that to take up ... It seems to me that with the show people there's always going to be this problem of ... [having] to run a generator, and that is always going to depend on their will to use that technology.

Q said:

> It's all right having CD-ROMS out there, but in reality they don't all have CD-ROM, not the player ... It's the CDI; it's the hardware. It works maybe, but how many of those families have got access to that? They don't have it, so there has to be something within the materials, within the support system, that motivates. So that's what we're working on at the moment. I think if we get that right then distance learning stands a better chance.

On the subject of competing priorities, O observed:

> There's quite a lot of projects for distance learning, but they've tended to be where they piloted the project with the school and produced distance learning. But the final outcome is not the distance learning material; it's the training material for the teachers in the school. So one of the most recent projects with EFECOT money – that was the outcome which I think, to some of us on the ground, [we] were a wee bit aggravated about. Because the final outcome was this wonderful big training pack, which was really great, but if I go into school with only a couple of children they don't want to know about producing distance learning materials absolutely precisely. They just want to get that child some work and send them off.

E said:

> I think one of the energies and one of the attractions around the kind of pump priming funding from Europe is that it has given us the chance to explore some options. But of course the down side of that is ... [that] you also set up a degree of expectation in the families and children and schools that if there isn't any long-term planning or funding coming in behind those which actually dashes those expectations and can be quite damaging.

But they recognised that such projects were vital to develop the educational technologies that would enhance Travellers' learning opportunities and outcomes. For example:

> The system is not there for distance learning to work, and that's what we're doing in one of our European projects – is working on the system so that families know what support there is there for the distance learning when they're travelling and how to get those packs and what to do. (Interview Q)

Involvement in EFECOT projects gave them a vision of future use of ICT:

> ... if we can develop ideas that we can use interactive IT to interest and involve children – ... it's a culture now for young people to actually use computers – to sit there in front of them. But if this can actually be inculcated into a teaching tool, having interactive pages, having links with their schools, with their teachers, with Traveller Education Services. Traveller Education Services being able to communicate over great distances to other counties to support the children. Immediate support for chil-

dren that here, at the end of this computer, you click on – you might not be able to speak to me, but at least you can send me an e-mail, and I can reply to you, instead of having to wait for me to turn up next week. (Interview A)

TESS staff members' partnerships with Traveller students and families, base schools and EFECOT have made significant contributions to the transformations of practice when technologies are aligned with the Travellers' and the TESS members' mobile itineraries; the possibilities for future learning are exciting:

Whether in the future through modern technology we can start on that sort of collaborative road with Travellers I don't know. I think it's probably a long way in the future. But I think the Internet could be a really good tool for us if we can only harness it and make it available to our people ... I think we've got a long way to go, but it's something that could be. Brave new world. (Interview S)

Implications for practice

ICT is reshaping the educational methods used by TESSs. Digital cameras have long been used to create personalised reading materials. As the development of resources for the whole school curriculum has become more sophisticated, compact disks and interactive sites have become widespread alongside the storybooks, topic files and photo-packs created by services. TESSs working as dispersed teams across large geographical areas maintain regular contact with one another through laptops and e-mail. However, it is the development of distance learning for Traveller children based on ICT that has had the most dramatic impact.

A number of TESSs first started experimenting with distance learning about twenty years ago, provoked initially by the travelling patterns of the Showmen. After spending two or three months at their winter quarters, where the children could attend school, the fairground families set out shortly before Easter for their travelling season. The time spent at each location from then until November varies from three or four days to about two weeks. Moving from school to school, week after week is rarely satisfactory, though the only option for some. Parents who had that experience described wasted years when they felt they learned nothing and wanted better for their children. So TESS teams in cooperation with the schools local to the Showmen's winter bases devised distance learning schemes, which sought to provide continuity through the travelling season.

Parental involvement and support in the children's learning is, as we have seen (Chapter 4), crucial. The learning packs presented a new challenge. Usually success in distance learning depends on the learner's motivation, reasonable literacy skills, ability to be an independent learner, and prompt and regular feedback. None of these could be guaranteed with the Traveller children, so the learning packs had to be tailored to the interests and capabilities of each child. In the early days of paper-based packs of work, feedback was always a problem, because it depended first on the families sending work back to school and then on teachers finding time to mark and return it. Frustration arose on both sides, which TESS teachers worked hard to alleviate.

Many TESSs included cassette tapes of instructions and videos offering extension material in the packs, but there were difficulties with batteries and often no electricity at convenient times for doing the work. TESSs in one region experimented with using fax machines. Parents were encouraged to take completed work into post offices or schools to fax back to their base schools, and to use mobile phones to keep in contact. At least one TESS arranged a video-conferencing session for a child to talk with her English teacher back at the base school about GCSE course work. All kinds of imaginative ideas and approaches were tried, but only on a small scale owing to the scarcity of resources.

In the 1990s EFECOT gave some TESSs the chance to take part in pilot projects to improve distance learning for fairground and circus children using new technologies. European funded projects, TOPILOT, FLEX and TRAPEZE linked a number of English TESSs with partners across Europe in experimental work with CDI players, satellite transmission systems and virtual classrooms, which caught the imaginations of the families involved, motivated the children and moved distance learning to a new phase of development. Showmen have always kept abreast of new technology and many of the parents who participated in the project quickly appreciated the advantages of ICT, beyond the immediate goal of education for their children. It brought some of them back to education themselves.

However, these projects, which raised the expectations of many families, were only pilot projects and could not be sustained in the same form beyond the project funding and timescale. The number of children who could benefit directly was limited and some families felt left out when the pilot phases did not lead to full implementation of the schemes. And only relatively few TESSs could be partners in the projects – those that had the staffing levels and established practice to enable them to carry out the project. But it was important to persist because, as the years went on, many Showmen were extending their travelling seasons for economic reasons and the time the children spent back at the base schools was diminishing.

TESS teachers were pioneers in developing these systems of distance learning for school-age children and overcoming the technical and operational difficulties. ICT is used regularly now by local authorities with other groups of learners who for some reason, are outside school but most of these schemes have the advantage of a fixed base for the child and a constant electricity supply. Working with mobile groups is much more complicated. It is unrealistic to expect TESS teams working within their current remit and resources to develop comprehensive, sustainable distance learning projects for all the Traveller children whose circumstances would benefit from them. Yet these approaches, especially using advanced mobile phone technology, could be highly effective extensions of mainstream schooling if placed within a national infrastructure of funding and support.

Therefore the DfES funding for the latest distance learning developments, the E-LAMP projects, is welcome. These are in their fourth phase now and involve about a dozen TESSs. It is also good to see that children and families from other Traveller groups, whose circumstances and travelling patterns make it possible, have been included. E-LAMP3 extended the remit to include secondary schools and children at the transfer stage, when it is so important for them to have support in moving to their new schools.

After the parents and children receive training from school staff and TESS teachers, they are presented with a laptop computer and a GPRS data card to enable Internet access. Schoolwork is put onto the computer, where it can be done on screen and then e-mailed back to school, enabling prompt feedback from the teacher. Further work can be downloaded as required. In these early, experimental years there have been connectivity problems because of slow transfer rates and communications blackspots, but motivation has increased. The costs – of computer hardware, telephone charges and staff time to work with families and schools to create the appropriate work – are being analysed. It will probably be expensive but, as recent evaluation reports have shown, of potentially enormous benefit to those children who are enabled to maintain their contact with education and become ICT literate in addition to improving other skills. It requires full commitment from families, TESSs, schools and the DfES to sustain and develop the projects further.

ICT literacy means access to learning for mobile people anywhere. Free access is available through libraries, youth and community centres and an increasing number of other locations. For Travellers to know that the facilities exist, how to access them and how to look at the content will be of immense value to them. Traveller children can be given ICT literacy through mainstream schooling and distance learning. The power of ICT is that it can extend mainstream learning into every part of the community. It is a tool for choice that should be available to every Traveller child.

Conclusion

The unique skills TESS teachers bring to their work should be acknowledged and celebrated. But the huge difficulties they face in practice – not always helped by current policies – cannot be denied.

We conclude with a checklist of principal points that we hope to have made in this book. Alongside the 26 teachers and heads of service from the nineteen TESSs who participated in the research, we have journeyed through five locations that are crucial to their work: the TESSs themselves; Traveller sites; government and LEAs; schools; and sites of innovative curriculum practice. We have sought to analyse their narratives and relate them to the literature. We have also outlined the implications for practice by the educators who are responsible for teaching Traveller children.

Throughout our account we focused on the intersection between the professional and the personal identities of TESS staff and their strategies to maximise Traveller children's learning outcomes. The identities and the strategy depend on each other to function effectively.

Traveller education literature has shifted in its representations of Travellers over the past 40 years from *deficit* to *disadvantage* to *difference* to *diversity*. But the fundamental ambivalence towards Travellers and the resilience of sedentarism (McVeigh, 1997) persist. The contemporary focus on diversity is both anti-sedentarist (Danaher *et al*, 2004) and anti-essentialist (Danaher, 2001b).

The words of TESS staff reported and analysed here indicate this conceptual shift. Several participants who had worked in Traveller education for a long time noted important changes in both official and unofficial attitudes towards Travellers' rights and their contributions to British culture and the economy. But there was also evidence of the resilience of sedentarist assumptions, even by some of the interviewees, suggesting that growth in understanding is not always in synch with formal statements such as legislation and policies.

We drew as appropriate on other writings on Traveller education to analyse the data constituted by the respondents' words, and linked what they said with their professional work and identities and the specific educational strategies adopted for teaching Traveller children. We also visited literature on teachers' work, to link the words of TESS staff with those of other educators. We wanted to look at wider educational practice in the early 21st century, to contextualise TESS practice.

Traveller education has been presented as a marginalised and politicised field within the complex and contested teaching profession. TESS staff members are marginalised partly because they work with Travellers. However, they can capitalise on ambivalent spaces in their work to foster understanding of Travellers and their educational abilities and needs. Their special position endorses the '... overt call for greater recognition of the important role that teachers have in building, managing and enhancing students' learning lives' (Loughran and Kelchtermans, 2006b, p109).

This study supports the argument that: 'Certainly it is vital that the task of researching and interrogating the links between work and identities in the lives of educators – whether marginalised pedagogues or otherwise – continues and expands' (Anteliz *et al*, 2006b, p756).

The book has shown the huge range of skills, expertise and knowledge required by TESS heads of service and teachers, which they use on a daily basis. Few other teachers have to maintain so many interconnected relationships, as explored in this book. It is the strength of these relationships that makes TESSs effective.

The good practice of working in close collaboration with Gypsy and Traveller families described in Chapter 4 should be maintained even as TESS staff assume more advisory and training roles. The training and professional development of others needs to be based on solid relationships with Traveller families and experience of proven strategies for teaching and learning.

In many parts of the country, education has been the pioneering service within local authorities in engaging supportively with Gypsies and Travellers to promote inclusion and counter prejudice. It has led the way for other services, such as health, the police and social services. The development of inter-agency work, described in Chapters 5 and 6, illustrates the positive outcome of early work by TESSs. As multi-agency work develops in the burgeoning Children's Centres, TESS staff will work with all service providers as well as teachers (see Siraj-Blatchford *et al*, 2007).

TESS staff have also engaged in pioneering work in other areas, notably in the development of distance learning for school aged Traveller children (see Chapter 10). Such work, however, cannot be sustained or expanded without realistic funding from central and local government. Funding and commitment are necessary for appropriate provision for students and the professional development of TESS staff. While we celebrate the achievements of TESS heads of service and teachers and observe how they are moving to new phases of work, we are aware that much more still needs to be done, and how much commitment and goodwill is required, to include Traveller children fully in the mainstream of education.

Finally, we hope that this book contributes to the debate about the roles and responsibilities of TESSs in Traveller education. Other stakeholders, including Travellers themselves, headteachers and teachers in schools and officers of other services in local authorities, can all do much to improve the educational opportunities for Traveller families. But TESS staff make unique and indispensable contributions to the educational lives of Traveller children, as this book has shown.

We hope that it has also demonstrated some of the characteristics of Anyanwu's (1998) definition of transformative research:

> Transformative research is a systematic enquiry into the real conditions which create oppression or hinder self-determination. It produces reflective knowledge which helps people to identify their situation and in doing so, to change such [a] situation for the better. In this regard, transformative research plays the important role of supporting the reflective process that promotes positive change. (p45)

In particular, we wish that this examination of the challenging and innovative work of TESS heads of service and teachers does indeed 'promote positive change' in the educational outcomes of Travellers and in the work and identities of the people who teach them.

References

Adams, B. and Smith, D. M. (1967) *Gipsies and education. In Children and their primary schools: The Plowden Report (Vol. 2: Research and surveys)* (pp595-600). London: HMSO

Anteliz, E. A., Coombes, P. N. and Danaher, P. A. (eds) (2006a) Marginalised pedagogues?: International studies of the work and identities of contemporary educators teaching 'minority' learners. *Theme issue of Teaching and Teacher Education*, 22(7), 753-837

Anteliz, E. A., Coombes, P. N. and Danaher, P. A. (2006b) Guest editors' introduction to special theme issue: Marginalised pedagogues? *Teaching and Teacher Education*, 22(7), 753-758

Anyanwu, C. N. (1998) Transformative research for the promotion of nomadic education in Nigeria. *Journal of Nomadic Studies*, 1, 44-51

Bhopal, K. with Gundara, J., Jones, C. and Owen, C. (2000) *Working towards inclusive education: Aspects of good practice for Gypsy Traveller children* (Research report RR238). Norwich, UK: Department for Education and Employment

Binns, D. (1990) History and growth of Traveller education. *British Journal of Educational Studies*, 38(3), 251-258

Blair, M. and Bourne, J. with Coffin, C., Creese, A. and Kenner, C. (1998) *Making the difference: Teaching and learning strategies in successful multi-ethnic schools* (DfEE research report RR59). London and Milton Keynes, UK. Department for Education and Employment and the Open University

Blaney, B. (2005) Towards success in secondary schooling. In C. Tyler (ed), *Traveller education: Accounts of good practice* (pp105-113). Stoke on Trent: Trentham Books

Bowen, P. (2001) English canal-boat children and the education issue 1900-1940: Towards a concept of traveller education? *History of Education*, 30(4), 359-378

Brunetti, G. J. (2006) Resilience under fire: Perspectives on the work of experienced, inner city high school teachers in the United States. *Teaching and Teacher Education*, 22(7), 812-825

Currie, H. (2006) 'Minorities', 'margins', 'misfits' and 'mainstreams'. *Teaching and Teacher Education*, 22(7), 835-837

Currie, H. and Danaher, P. A. (2001) Government funding for English Traveller Education Support Services. *Multicultural Teaching*, 19(2), 33-36

Danaher, G. R., Coombes, P. N., Simpson, J., Harreveld, R. E. and Danaher, P. A. (2002) From double agents to double vision: Marginalisation and potential transformation among three groups of open and distance teachers. *ODLAA Occasional Papers*, 12-25

Danaher, P. A. (2001a) Learning on the run: Traveller education for itinerant show children in coastal and western Queensland. Unpublished PhD thesis, Faculty of Education and Creative Arts, Central Queensland University, Rockhampton, Qld

Danaher, P. A. (2001b) The researcher as occupational Traveller: From strategic essentialism to creative understanding. *Journal of Nomadic Studies*, 4, 66-78

Danaher, P. A. (2005) From constructive solutions to creative dissent: Economies of performance and ecologies of practice among English headteachers of Travellers. Paper presented at the annual conference of the Australian Association for Research in Education, Parramatta Campus, University of Western Sydney, Sydney, NSW

Danaher, P. A., Moriarty, B. J. and Danaher, G. R. (2004) Three pedagogies of mobility for Australian show people: Teaching about, through and towards the questioning of sedentarism. *Melbourne Studies in Education*, 45(2), 47-66

Day, C., Stobart, G., Sammons, P. and Kington, A. (2006) Variations in the work and lives of teachers: Relative and relational effectiveness. *Teachers and Teaching: Theory and Practice,* 12(2), 169-192

Denning, P. (2004) Building a culture of innovation. *Ubiquity*, 5(8), 1-13. Retrieved May 31, 2004, from http://www.acm.org/ubiquity/interviews/v5i8_denning.html

Department for Education and Skills (2003) *Aiming high: Raising the achievement of Gypsy and Traveller pupils.* London: DfES

Department for Education and Skills (2005) *Higher standards, better schools for all: More choice for parents and pupils* (Schools White Paper 2005. Cm6677). London: DfES

Department for Education and Skills (2006) *Positive pathways for the future of provision for Gypsy, Roma and Traveller children – a guide to good practice.* London: DfES

Department of Education and Science (1967) *Children and their primary schools: The Plowden Report.* London: HMSO

Department of Education and Science (1981) *DES circular 1/81, Education Act 1980: Admission to schools, appeals, publications of information and school attendance orders.* London: DES

Department of Education and Science (1983) *The education of Travellers' children: An HMI discussion paper.* London: DES

Department of Education and Science (1985) *Education for all: The report of the Committee of Inquiry into the Education of Children from Ethnic Minority Groups: The Swann Report.* London: HMSO

Derrington, C. (2005) Perceptions of behaviour and patterns of exclusion: Gypsy Traveller students in English secondary schools. *Journal of Research in Special Educational Needs*, 5(2), 55-61

Derrington, C. and Kendall, S. (2004) *Gypsy Traveller students in secondary schools: Culture, identity and achievement.* Stoke on Trent: Trentham Books

Devon Traveller Education Service and Marjon TV (1993) *Between two worlds* [video recording]. Torquay, UK: Devon Learning Resources

Doyle, M. E. and Smith, M. K. (2001) Classical leadership. *The Encyclopedia of Informal Education.* Retrieved January 7, 2007, from http://www.infed.org/leadership/traditional_leadership.htm

Dyer, C. (ed) (2006) *The education of nomadic peoples: Current issues, future prospects.* New York: Berghahn Books

Ellsmore, S. (2005) *Carry on, teachers! Representations of the teaching profession in screen culture.* Stoke on Trent: Trentham Books

Foster, W. P. (1989) Toward a critical practice of leadership. In J. Smyth (ed), *Critical perspectives on educational leadership* (pp39-62). London: Falmer Press

Gale, T. C. and Densmore, K. (2003) *Engaging teachers: Towards a radical democratic agenda for schooling.* Maidenhead, UK: Open University Press

Giddens, A. (1984) *The constitution of society: Outline of the theory of structuration.* Cambridge, UK: Polity Press

Gillborn, D. and Gipps, C. (1996) *Recent research on the achievement of ethnic minority pupils*. London: Ofsted

Gobbo, F. (2006) Along the margins, across the borders: Teaching and learning among Veneto *attrazionisti viaggianti* in Italy. *Teaching and Teacher Education*, 22(7), 788-803

Gouwens, J. A. (2001) *Migrant education: A reference handbook*. Santa Barbara, CA: ABC-Clio

Hall, C. (2004) Theorising changes in teachers' work. *Canadian Journal of Educational Administration and Policy*, 32. Retrieved May 27, 2005, from http://www.umanitoba.ca/publications/cjeap/articles/noma/theorising.change.html

Harreveld, R. E. (2002) Broking changes: A study of power and identity through discourses. Unpublished PhD thesis, Faculty of Education and Creative Arts, Central Queensland University, Rockhampton, Qld

Hatch, K. (2006) Traveller children: Have laptop will travel. *The Teacher*, 24

Henderson, R. W. (2005) The social and discursive construction of itinerant farm workers' children as literacy learners. Unpublished PhD thesis, School of Education, James Cook University of North Queensland, Townsville, Qld

HMSO (2004) *The Children Act*. London: HMSO. Retrieved December 17, 2006, from http://www.opsi.gov.uk/acts/acts2004/20040031.htm

Johnson, D. W. and Johnson, R. T. (1008) The three Cs of effective schools: Cooperative community, constructive conflict, civic values. *Connections*, 5(1), 4-10

Jordan, E. S. (2000) The exclusionary comprehensive school system: The experience of Showground families in Scotland. *International Journal of Educational Research*, 33(3), 253-263

Kenny, M. (1997) *The routes of resistance: Travellers and second-level schooling*. Aldershot, UK: Ashgate Publishing

Kiddle, C. (1981) *What shall we do with the children?* Barnstaple, UK: Spindlewood

Kiddle, C. (1999) *Traveller children: A voice for themselves*. London: Jessica Kingsley Publishers

Kiddle, C. (2000) Partnerships depend on power-sharing: An exploration of the relationships between Fairground and Gypsy Traveller parents and their children's teachers in England. *International Journal of Educational Research*, 33(3), 265-274

Kiddle, C. (2004) Leading and managing a dispersed team to provide an effective Traveller Education Support Service. Unpublished Master of Education dissertation, School of Education and Lifelong Learning, Exeter University, Exeter, UK

Leaton Gray, S. (2006) *Teachers under siege*. Stoke on Trent: Trentham Books

LeBlanc Flores, J. (ed) (1996) *Children of la frontera: Binational efforts to serve Mexican migrant and immigrant students*. Charleston, WV: Clearinghouse on Rural Education and Small Schools

Liégeois, J.-P. (1998) *School provision for ethnic minorities: The Gypsy paradigm* (2nd ed) (trans. by S. ni Shuinéar). Paris and Hatfield, UK: Gypsy Research Centre, Université René Descartes and University of Hertfordshire Press

Lloyd, G. and Stead, J. (2001) 'The boys and girls not calling me names and the teachers to believe me': Name calling and the experiences of Travellers in school. *Children and Society*, 15, 361-374

Loughran, J. and Kelchtermans, G. (eds) (2006a) Teachers' lives. *Theme issue of Teachers and Teaching: Theory and Practice*, 12(1), 105-209

Loughran, J. and Kelchtermans, G. (2006b) Editorial: Teachers' work lives. *Teachers and Teaching: Theory and Practice*, 12(1), 107-109

Lucassen, L., Willems, W. and Cottar, A. (1998) Introduction. In L. Lucassen, W. Willems and A. Cottar (eds), *Gypsies and other itinerant groups: A socio-historical approach* (pp1-13). Houndmills, UK: Macmillan

Marks, K. (2003) EFECOT: Supporting the Travelling tradition. In J. Bradley (ed), *The open classroom: Distance learning in and out of schools* (pp67-83). London: Kogan Page

Marks, K. (2004) *Traveller education: Changing times, changing technologies.* Stoke on Trent: Trentham Books

Marks, K. (2005) Developments in supported distance learning. In C. Tyler (ed), *Traveller education: Accounts of good practice* (pp121-134). Stoke on Trent: Trentham Books

McDougall, J. K. (2004) Changing mindsets: A study of Queensland primary teachers and the visual literacy initiative. Unpublished PhD thesis, Faculty of Education and Creative Arts, Central Queensland University, Rockhampton, Qld

McVeigh, R. (1997) Theorising sedentarism: The roots of anti-nomadism. In T. Acton (ed), *Gypsy politics and Traveller identity* (pp7-25). Hatfield, UK: University of Hertfordshire Press

Mott, G. (2000) *Refugees and asylum seekers: The role of LEAs* (EMIE report no. 59). Slough, UK: Education Management Information Exchange, National Foundation for Educational Research

National Association of Teachers of Travellers (1996) *The Smiths.* Wolverhampton, UK: NATT

Ofsted (1996) *The education of Travelling children: A report from the office of Her Majesty's Chief Inspector of Schools.* London: Ofsted

Ofsted (1999) *Raising the attainment of minority ethnic pupils: School and LEA responses.* London: Ofsted

Ofsted (2003) *Provision and support for Traveller pupils.* London: Ofsted

O'Hanlon, C. and Holmes, P. (2004) *The education of Gypsy and Traveller children: Towards inclusion and educational achievement.* Stoke on Trent: Trentham Books

Reiss, C. (1975) *Education of travelling children.* London: Macmillan

Rowan, L. O. (2001) *Write me in: Inclusive texts in the primary classroom.* Newtown, NSW: Primary English Teachers Association

Saunders, P., Clarke, J., Kendall, S., Lee, A., Lee, S. and Matthews, F. (2000) *Gypsies and Travellers in their own words: Words and pictures of travelling life. Leeds*, UK: Leeds Traveller Education Service

Siraj-Blatchford, I., Clarke, K. and Needham, M. (eds) (2007) *The team around the child: Multi-agency working in the early years.* Stoke on Trent: Trentham Books

Somekh, B. and Lewin, C. (eds) (2005) *Research methods in the social sciences.* London: Sage Publications

Sullivan, B. (2006) A living theory of a practice of social justice: Realising the right of Traveller children to educational equality. Unpublished PhD thesis, Department of Education and Professional Studies, University of Limerick, Limerick, Ireland

Tyler, C. (ed) (2005) *Traveller education: Accounts of good practice.* Stoke on Trent: Trentham Books

Weafer, J. A. (2001) *The education and accommodation needs of Travellers in the Archdiocese of Dublin.* Dublin, Ireland: Crosscare

Wood, M. (2005) 'Literacy for All' and other curriculum partnerships at Key Stage 2. In C. Tyler (ed), *Traveller education: Accounts of good practice* (pp81-90). Stoke on Trent: Trentham Books

Woods, P. and Jeffrey, B. (2002) The reconstruction of primary teachers' identities. *British Journal of Sociology of Education*, 23(1), 89-106

Index